LIVE IT!

LIVE IT!

ACHIEVE SUCCESS
BY LIVING WITH PURPOSE

JAIREK ROBBINS

GRAND
HARBOR
PRESS

Published by Grand Harbor Press, Grand Haven, MI
www.brilliancepublishing.com

Amazon, the Amazon logo, and Grand Harbor Press are trademarks of Amazon.com, Inc., or its affiliates.

ISBN-13: 9781477824740
ISBN-10: 147782474X
LCCN: 2014935933
Cover design by FaceoutStudio

To my mom, dad, grandparents,
and the village it took to shape me
into the man I am today!

Contents

FOREWORD

The first time I met Jairek Robbins, I could tell I had met someone special. He exuded that unique gift of contagious passion that many speak about, but few fully live. Fortunately, he's now written a book that will enable you to tap into your latent potential as well.

Jairek's concept of *Learn it, Live it, Give it* is simple yet powerful when put in motion. When looking back over my own journey, I can clearly see the ways in which this *learn, live, give* philosophy parallels the steps I took along the way.

As a kid, I wanted nothing more than a successful Wall Street career. But while traveling as a college student, I met a young boy begging on the streets of India. When I asked him what he wanted most in the world, he simply answered, "a pencil." As I handed him a pencil and watched his eyes light up with possibility, I knew that my life had been permanently altered. We each have these unique moments that have the potential to transform our life's journey, and this was undoubtedly one of mine.

I eventually left a job at Bain & Company to launch Pencils of Promise with twenty-five dollars just before my twenty-fifth birthday. The organization has now built hundreds of schools around the world, educated thousands of children, and delivered millions of educational hours. But when I consider the process of turning my big idea into reality, it's clear that the steps Jairek has laid out capture the most important elements that I wish someone had told me from the start.

There are many books written by inspiring individuals, but this book is an absolute standout. It will help you define an ideal vision for your life and then challenge you to take action. Jairek writes with honesty and integrity, sharing moments of intense vulnerability that demonstrate how every one of us must push through our greatest challenges to become our most aspirational self.

Every day is a new opportunity to make your life a story worth telling. This book will provide you with the ambition and ability to craft an extraordinary journey ahead. I hope you choose to live with meaning and purpose, and may the words on the pages ahead guide you along the way.

Adam Braun
www.AdamBraun.com
www.pencilsofpromise.org

INTRODUCTION

In December 2003, I was living as a volunteer in Kangulumira, a rural Ugandan farming village, when I was told I had only five days left to live.

I was forced to confront in that moment the reality of my life, not the "someday" goals and loose plans I had made, but how I had actually lived my life up to that point. The choices I made, the priorities I set, and what I had to show for myself. If I were to die in a few days, would I die feeling satisfied and content with my life? Would I die knowing that I had lived a life that was truly worth living? Did I give back and make the difference that I was created to make?

I had lived a full life up until that point and had achieved many of the dreams and goals that I had come up with thus far. I was twenty-three years old. I had climbed the Great Wall of China, visited the Taj Mahal in India, gone diving with great white sharks in South Africa, and spent over a hundred days on a ship circumnavigating the world. I was a typical young adult who thought I had it all figured out, but I still always felt like something was missing.

Why wasn't I 100 percent happy and content with my life?

I suppose I had come to this realization earlier but had pushed the thoughts aside while I slowly chipped away, trying to make a little progress. I was actively looking for ways to improve myself and grow. I spent a summer working at a lumberyard in Vancouver, Canada, learning how to fall in love with hard work. I traveled to developing countries and experienced what it was like to live without running water, electricity, or toilets, learning how to fall in love with life in its simplest form.

In Kangulumira, I got malaria, and I was now facing one of the most challenging moments of my life. As far as I could tell, there were only a few options:

1. Give up, tap out, and die.

2. Cross my fingers and hope something good happens.

3. Find a reason to live and fight like hell.

I am not one to just give up on something, especially my life, so the first option didn't sit well with me. The crossed-finger method seemed like a scary option, because I wouldn't be in control of my own destiny. This left me with the only option that made sense—find a reason to live and fight like hell!

I spent the next few days digging for a purpose that I felt would make my life worth living. Up until that day, I believed my purpose in life was coaching. I had helped hundreds of people make more money, lose weight, find fulfilling relationships, and achieve all kinds of other results. All of this was wonderful, but it lacked the depth I was searching for in the long run.

When faced with my own impending death, I discovered that my ultimate goal and purpose in life was to inspire more people to focus on giving back and making a valuable difference in the world. Most people are so consumed with trying to hit their own personal goals, however, that helping others always gets pushed to the back burner. Many people I talked to wanted to find a way to achieve more success in their lives so that they could finally find the love they were searching for and eventually give back in a meaningful way. (What I find ironic is that if people would spend more time giving back in a meaningful way and sharing the love they already have with others, they would realize how successful they already are.)

I spent countless hours lecturing friends, trying to convince them to spend their lives focused on giving back and easing up on their never-ending quest for success. After months of frustration, I got to a point where I realized that I was fighting an uphill battle that I was never going to win. If I wanted to get through to people, I would have to change my approach.

I remember hearing a quote attributed to actor Jim Carrey: "I think everybody should get rich and famous and do everything they ever dreamed of so they can see that it's not the answer." I realized I needed to help people speed up the process of achieving the success they were after so they could get to Carrey's conclusion through firsthand experience. When they reached their goals and felt better able to start giving back, the effect would be exponential.

I sum up this process in three simple parts: Learn it, Live it, Give it.

- Learn it—Learn all that you need to design your ideal vision for your life.

- Live it—Apply all that you've learned to achieve the results you desire and deserve.

- Give it—Find a way to pay it forward and help others do the same.

This book will teach you how to apply this process to your life and work. It will guide you through designing your ideal vision for your life and walk you through the tools that will help you turn that dream into reality faster than you could ever imagine. This formula is fresh, new, and more effective than anything you've tried before.

I have only one request—play full out and pay it forward!

CHAPTER 1:

IDEAL DAY VISION

W hat if you were able to design your dream life?

Instead of waiting to see what life has in store for you, imagine creating a vision for exactly what your ideal life would be like and manifesting that vision into reality. This dream life would be so fulfilling, rich, and abundant that you wouldn't trade it for anything on earth. No amount of money, fame, or recognition could ever be better than being able to live that day-to-day life.

I can tell you from personal experience that making your dream life a reality is better than you could ever imagine! In this book, I will teach you a proven step-by-step process to transform your current life into the one of your dreams.

The first step in making that vision a reality is to design your *ideal vision* for your life.

After working with thousands of clients, I'll warn you that thinking about your ideal life vision as a whole is too big of a bite to start with. It's overwhelming. Instead, let's start with something a bit more reasonable: your vision for the ideal day. This isn't a silly fantasy or another goal-setting exercise; creating a vision for your ideal day will become the linchpin for transforming your day-to-day reality.

I developed this process when I needed to make some major improvements in my life, and I learned through my own experience how powerful it can be. This simple process helped me go from working my butt off at three different jobs and barely making enough money to pay my bills to living the life of my dreams. That may sound strange to some people who know who my dad is, and who think I've had it easy my whole life. My dad always had one rule when it came to money: "I'll help you get through college, but after that, don't ask." In hindsight, this is the best gift he could have ever given me, because it made me become self-reliant. I knew that if I wanted to live the life of my dreams, I needed to create it, instead of having it handed to me.

After years of hard work, I can now say I made my dreams a reality. I travel the world as a coach and speaker, inspiring others to live their dreams and teaching them how to manifest their dream lives. This is my passion and I wouldn't trade it for anything. The Ideal Day exercise was the foundation for me making that powerful change. But I don't just know from personal experience that it works. I have used it to help thousands of people around the world transform their health, relationships, and businesses, and most importantly, begin to live the day-to-day experiences that they *love*.

It's worked for me and my clients, and now it can work for you!

The reason why this exercise becomes a springboard for transforming your life is that it gets to the root of what you truly desire, even if you don't currently realize you have those feelings. By closely examining your Ideal Day vision, it becomes easier to

identify the areas of your life that are on track and th
hindering the end results you are striving for.

Over the years, it's easy for people to slip into au
get stuck doing things they think they *need* to do versus things
that they have always *wanted* to do. When they take a step back
and examine how their actions make them feel, most people realize there are changes they could make that could impact their
happiness now and in the future. The goal of the Ideal Day exercise is to illuminate the gaps between where you are today and
where you want to be. As soon as you have that information, the
rest of the book teaches you how to make the changes necessary
to transform your current reality into your dream life.

Before going through this process, my life felt like a constant
race of pursuing accomplishment after accomplishment. No matter how many experiences or successes I was able to achieve, I
always thought, "What's next? Where do I go from here? How
do I get there?" I never felt settled or fulfilled inside, since I was
always in the mind-set that there was something else I had to do
before I could *really* enjoy my life.

So I sat down and went through the Ideal Day process, and
I came up with the most magnificent ideal day I had ever imagined for myself. This day would be so fulfilling and enjoyable
that I could make it my day-to-day reality and become the happiest, healthiest, and most fulfilled version of myself. This is the
type of day you will be imagining for yourself. Now I must warn
you, for those of you who are thinking the perfect day consists
of piña coladas and lying on a tropical beach all day, think again.
That day might sound refreshing right now, but once you get
there and spend a few days back-to-back doing nothing, you'll
get bored. While it might sound nice to figure that out from
experience, I can assure you that it will leave you feeling empty,
frustrated, and wondering why it isn't what you thought it would
be. There are only a few things that bring consistent fulfillment

into people's lives, and this exercise will guide you through the process of including them in your Ideal Day vision. In my own personal development, experience, and education in psychology, I have learned that the only way to feel fulfilled in the long run is through *growth* and *contribution.*

According to my friend Brendon Burchard in his book *The Millionaire Messenger*, there are three questions you will have to answer at the end of your life:

1. Did I live fully?

2. Did I love openly?

3. Did I matter?[1]

The goal of my book is to lead you toward a life of growth and contribution, where you can answer yes to these questions every day of your life.

A Clearer Perspective

In 2011, I was introduced to a potential client for one-on-one coaching. The e-mail introduction let me know that he was incredibly successful, well connected, and looking for someone that could help him expand his personal and professional vision. During our first conversation, he let me know that he was not looking for someone to help him simply set goals and go after more results. He was already a pro at that and had been quite successful over the years.

He gave me a brief history of his life. After graduating from an Ivy League school, he decided to take a job that offered a promising financial future, instead of pursuing a job he was passionate about. When the company went bankrupt years later and he was faced with another major career decision, again his head and his heart wouldn't align. He felt pulled toward options that would make a meaningful difference in the world, but he ended up taking a position at a top banking firm that would help him create a secure financial future for himself and his future family.

He had been working there for roughly nine years when we met, and during that time he worked his way up the corporate ladder. He was one rung away from becoming a managing partner in the company, which was the highest position a person could reach through promotion. With all of these amazing results he achieved, the career highlights that most people dream about, something just wasn't right. He was grateful for his successes but always felt like something was missing.

During our first conversation I walked him through the Ideal Day exercise and helped him design his ideal vision for his life. As he shared his vision with me, we noticed it was nothing like the day-to-day life he was currently living. At the time, he was waking up at five o'clock in the morning every day, hustling to the office in the city, working all day at his desk while answering constant phone calls and feeling pressured from the team to perform, wrapping up at seven o'clock in the evening or later, heading out to networking dinners to build relationships, and finally spending the last bits of the night with his wife preparing for the next day.

Over the next few years of working together, we were able to help him reshape his life. He transitioned from working nonstop in a career he was very good at but didn't find fulfilling to gaining a better work-life balance and starting his own business. He didn't even have to change industries to make this shift. Nowadays his life is quite different. He spends his mornings running on the beach, and his days working on the business he started from his home office with a gorgeous view of the countryside. His afternoons and evenings are filled with yoga, dinners with friends, and finding unique ways to grow and expand who he is as a man.

The Ideal Day vision enabled him to gain a clearer perspective on what is most important in his life, so that he could start working to make his actual life match the vision he created.

This is exactly what you will be doing next. This is much more than just a feel-good exercise. We are not trying to get you excited only about some future vision—we want you to make this vision so real that you can literally feel it in your body. The more certainty you can create when thinking of this vision, the faster you are going to be able to transform it from a vision to actual reality.

This mental rehearsal process has been proven to positively affect athletes and help increase their overall performance. We will be focusing on mental rehearsal later in the book. For now, let's just dive in and help you design your Ideal Day vision.

To get the most out of this exercise, first and foremost, you need to use your best effort. That should go without saying, but I wanted to mention it just in case you're thinking you've heard this before and can skim through this section to the next chapter. This book doesn't work like that. We are going through a specific process that builds on information in a linear fashion. If you skip an exercise, it's going to keep you from being able to participate in the next one. This is the foundation of the process. Just like building a house, you need to start with the foundation.

This exercise will take only twenty to thirty minutes, and it's best to do it from start to finish in one sitting. Make sure you are in a place where you will not be interrupted and that you have a pen and notebook to record your answers.

As you start imagining your ideal day, part of your vision might be a mirror image of your daily life, or very close to it. Other aspects might be so different that they seem worlds apart. Know that this is typical for most people and that the exercise will be valuable no matter how your dream compares to your current reality. The important part is to think hard about your ideal vision and record it. The following chapters will guide you through what to do with this information to start transforming your life.

When I guide my clients and audience members through the Ideal Day exercise in person, I always help them get mentally and physically prepared before we get started. Concentration, creativity, and enthusiasm are all important when coming up with your ideal vision. There are various tactics that work for people, so I included some ideas for you to consider.

Get loose. Stand up, jump around, stretch, and shake it out. Take five deep breaths from your diaphragm.

Studies have shown that certain body positions increase testosterone and decrease cortisol, leaving you feeling more confident.[2] Stand or sit in one of these *power poses* to make sure you don't hold back when you create your ideal vision. One example of a pose is the *Superman*. Stand tall with your hands on your hips, feet slightly apart. Think positive thoughts. Take a moment to remember a few past accomplishments and times you were happy.

Ideal Day Exercise

Imagine waking up on your ideal day, a day that would be extraordinary and magical. A day that would make you look back later and think it was the greatest day—not because of the "results" you were able to achieve, but instead, because of the type of person you were and the amazing life you were able to experience. This is a day that would leave you feeling excited and fulfilled.

Imagine waking up on the morning of your ideal day. Think about the mind-set you would have from the very first moment you open your eyes. How much energy, passion, joy, and excitement would you have for the day that was about to occur? Take a moment to set the scene in your mind. Picture the sights around you as you wake up on this perfect day. Maybe your loved one is in bed next to you, or a beautiful sunrise is shining in through the window. Think about how refreshed and well rested your mind and body feel.

As your thoughts start to focus on the day ahead of you, how would your morning play out? Maybe you would go for a run, spend quality time with your family, or relax with the newspaper and a cup of coffee. There are endless possibilities to how you might spend your morning, but focus on what would be most fulfilling to you on an ideal day in your future.

I go through this exercise in many of the workshops I teach, and I often ask participants to share their vision aloud. Since people have so many different versions of their Ideal Day vision, it can help to get a taste of the variety to spark your own imagination and creativity. I will share some of these examples to help you understand how others have responded to this exercise.

Recently, a man from Ireland who looked to be in his fifties described his ideal morning for our group to consider. He said his biggest focus would be on spending time with his family. Nothing would make him feel more fulfilled than to eat breakfast with his wife and daughter, and take his daughter to school. He wanted that quality time with his family more than anything else. His vision for his ideal morning was incredibly simple, but it showed how well he was able to home in on what would make him the happiest, day in and day out.

For others, their vision is laser focused on results. Stuart Allison, a chief master sergeant in the US Air Force, makes inspiring others a core part of his Ideal Day vision.[3] He leads and inspires a large and diverse organization, and he is passionate about motivating and developing his team so it can achieve greater success. When he thinks of the ideal way to start his day, he visualizes upholding the leadership qualities and attitudes that would be inspirational to those around him. In order to have the personal strength to do this, Allison also focuses on having optimal health and energy, both emotionally and physically. He pictures himself being fueled by exercise, nourished through healthy food, and living in a state of happiness and love.

Neither of these visions is right or wrong, or one better than the other. Ideal days are as unique as the people experiencing them. As you think about your own ideal day, know that your vision can be as grand or as simple as you like; just make sure whatever you include in this vision are things that will make you feel most alive.

As ideal morning turns into ideal afternoon, consider your mental and physical state, as well as your actions. How much natural, vibrant energy would you have in your body? Focus on the emotions that would drive that energy. Maybe you would feel passionate about your life, grateful, centered, and filled with love.

Imagine what you would do with your time on this perfect afternoon. Perhaps you would find a way to grow mentally, emotionally, and physically, learning and trying new things. This could be through work, volunteering, or hobbies. Maybe you would be the CEO of a big company, the owner of a small business, or doing some type of work or volunteering that is meaningful to you.

Maybe on this ideal day, it is all about travel and adventure. Perhaps you have figured out how to generate income while you are out exploring the world. If this is the case, imagine where you would go and what experiences you would want to partake in.

Identify whom you would spend time with on this ideal afternoon. Would you be with family, friends, talented colleagues, or all of the above? Or maybe you would spend some peaceful time alone.

Another client I've worked with, Janice De La Garza, a mother and a manager at an engineering and manufacturing firm, pictures herself going through her ideal day feeling strong, powerful, and as if she were capable of achieving anything she desired.[4] She sees herself being in full control of her emotions, rather than letting her emotions control her. On her ideal day, she envisions herself being surrounded by her family and a wonderful group of friends who support her in everything she does. She is loved, valued, and cherished for the person she is. She also makes it a point to spend time appreciating the people and animals in her life. As part of her ideal day, De La Garza pictures herself working as well as volunteering and giving back to people in need.

As you think about your ideal afternoon, make sure to include all of the elements that would be most fulfilling to you. Remember, anything is possible in this vision. Take time to brainstorm on all of the activities you've been wanting to do, but somehow never have time for in your day-to-day life. Maybe you've always wanted to become an expert glassblower, learn a new language, or start your own nonprofit organization. Or perhaps you just want to live in the moment and enjoy the beauty of the little things in life—the smiles, hugs, and kind words that make it all worthwhile.

As you head into the evening on this perfect day, think about how you would feel having accomplished so much in one day, whether tasks, goals, learning, growing, or just enjoying. Picture yourself bringing this positive energy into the end of your day. Would the perfect evening be spent with your family eating dinner and enjoying one another's company? Or maybe the evening would be quiet time to recharge after a busy and productive day. Take time to write down what your ideal evening would encompass.

Another person who has done this exercise envisions her perfect evening as a time to reconnect with the people she cares about. Victoria Boye, a freelance writer and mother, pictures herself preparing a wholesome meal for her husband and young son, and enjoying a lively conversation during dinner.[5] She sees the three of them playing in the backyard, then putting their son to sleep with a bedtime story and snuggle time. Afterward, she has quality one-on-one time with her husband and speaks on the phone to a friend or family member to catch up. The very end of her ideal day includes a little time alone reading in her personal library. All of these activities that Boye includes in her Ideal Day vision fulfill emotional needs and create a balanced life. Furthermore, throughout her whole day, she says she would celebrate the little things—the people around her and all of the positive things she was blessed with in life.

As you envision your ideal day coming to a close, what thoughts would be going through your head? Would you take the time to be grateful for having such an amazing day with people who mean so much to you? Perhaps you would reflect on your good health, or the positive impact you were able to make in the world that day. Maybe you would take the time to thank your family and friends for being there to support you, and tell them how much they truly mean to you. Take a moment and reflect.

If you were able to live one ideal day, what would happen if you were able to live two? What other amazing things would you do? Take the time to create a few different variations of your Ideal Day vision. I actually update my own personal vision at least once per year to ensure that if there are any adjustments needed from growing as a person or learning a new life lesson that it is updated accordingly.

Key Factors
Thinking back through your Ideal Day vision, what are the most important parts of that vision?

Which parts, if removed from your day, would cause it to no longer be your absolute ideal day?

How much of your ideal day was focused on your outlook and mind-set?

Summary
The goal of these action steps is to lay the mental and emotional foundation for the rest of this book and the process it outlines.

This exercise alone will not change your life. When I first developed the process of designing my Ideal Day vision, I thought about it, and I recorded it on paper. From there, I waited for amazing things to start happening. Then I waited some more. Finally, I realized that visualizing my ideal day and thinking about my ideal life and my ultimate goals weren't going to change anything; I had to take action.

The problem was that when I looked at my day-to-day life, it was not even close to my dream life. (After doing this exercise, I'm sure a lot of people can relate.) Being so far from where I wanted to be in life, I couldn't wrap my head around where to start making positive changes, which is why I didn't make any changes. Even though I knew a wealth of "self-help" tactics and tools, the knowledge wasn't translating to my actions in a way that made anything in my life improve. I also recognized that the fear of failing (or possibly even succeeding) left me stuck knowing what I really wanted but afraid of doing anything about it.

I realized the Ideal Day vision was only the beginning of a larger transformation process. Just knowing what you want is not good enough; you have to learn what steps to take to get what you want and apply that knowledge through action. I'm not talking about just a few actions here and there, but consistent daily action. I found that I needed to dedicate real effort and work toward making changes that would lead me closer to my ideal day and life.

I worked hard to come up with a process that helped me make important changes in my life. I started sharing it with others, and I found out it worked for them too.

LIVE IT CHALLENGE
Throughout this book, we will feature LIVE IT Challenges, which are actions you can take right away to make immediate improvements in your life.

Review your Ideal Day vision and read it aloud at least once a day for the next thirty days to help you stay laser focused.

Each day, find at least one new action you can take to move closer and closer to having your actual day become your ideal day—the one you created in your vision!

CHAPTER 2:

FOCUSING ON THE MAJORS

We are living at a point in time when prioritizing what's important in life has become challenging for people around the world. In a connected society, an endless stream of information makes it easy to get distracted from our goals and sucked into a world where materialism, self-image, and celebrity gossip take on a false sense of importance. People invest a lot of energy in thinking and caring about these concerns because it's easy, fun, or they feel pressured to do so, but in reality, it can be counterproductive to their happiness. Time spent on the trivial parts of life can be an escape from the real world, but it will never bring true fulfillment.

Focusing on the important parts of life is the foundation for success, which I learned at a young age from my father. This was the starting point that helped me turn my Ideal Day vision into reality. This chapter builds on the principles that have already proven effective for millions of people and takes a modern approach to tackling the majors in your own life. As we move forward in this book, you will use the majors you identify in this chapter to help guide you on your mission to live your ideal life. First, let's get specific and define the difference between a *major* and *minor* area of life.

The Majors—These are the aspects of your life that need to be in order before you can achieve the end results you are after. If you imagine building your dream house, you may envision how beautiful and luxurious it will be when it's finished, focusing on details like granite countertops and a giant deck out back. It's fun to imagine those details, but without the basic elements that go into building a house, like the internal structure, the roof, and plumbing, would you be content with just countertops and a deck? No. The same holds true in your life. The majors are the basic elements that build the foundation for your happiness and enable you to reach for bigger and better things.

You might be familiar with psychologist Abraham Maslow's hierarchy of needs, a theory that breaks down human needs into different levels of importance. The hierarchy is often depicted as a pyramid, where the top level can only be achieved when the needs on the levels below have been met. This model serves as a good example of the majors and minors. To reach your fullest potential at the top of the pyramid, you have to start with the fundamentals at the bottom.

The Minors—Appearing in an endless number of variations and differing from person to person, the minors can sometimes be hard to identify. One reason for this is that people typically enjoy a wide range of minor things. In fact, many people build their whole lives on the minors. It's easy to do this because unlike the majors, the minors are easy and they frequently offer instant gratification. They are distractions, vices, and otherwise less important activities that either tear down your foundation of the majors you've established or limit your progress on improving your foundation. When people focus on the minors, they tend to justify their actions by playing up the importance of those activities, saying they are a priority. For example, going shopping to find the perfect outfit for an upcoming party might seem like a nonnegotiable priority. In reality, that time and money could be spent in ways that would better support long-term happiness and reaching personal goals.

It's easy for people to fixate on the minors, because the minors can serve as a distraction—something to fill the void felt by not making progress on the majors. To avoid thinking about the hard work needed to close the gap between a person's real life and ideal life, people focus on these activities in the moment.

An Obsession with the Minors

Our society has become obsessed with minor things. Mass media, social media, and advertising have evolved over the years so that we are now inundated with messages about the minors. Keeping up with the Joneses can translate to an ongoing desire for purchasing the latest and greatest or having as much fun as Facebook says everyone else is having. Instead of staying focused on the major things necessary to reach our goals, distractions abound. The list of unhealthy indulgences we see people partaking in each and every day can go on and on, which is how some minors in life can start to seem like majors.

Adults are not the only people who get sucked into the minors; kids engage in this type of behavior at an early age as well. The average young person today in a country with a strong gamer culture will have spent ten thousand hours playing online games by the time he or she is twenty-one years old. That is comparable to the amount of time American children spend attending class from fifth grade through high school, if they have perfect attendance, according to Jane McGonigal, author of *Reality Is Broken*, in her TED talk.[1] If you've ever seen the emotional reaction of a young person who has invested hours and even days of their life reaching a certain level on a video game, only to have it suddenly shut off, you know it's more than just a game to them. It has become reality. Many young people have chosen virtual games over their lives in the real world. Instead of focusing on the majors, they spend time escaping reality.

Where do they learn this behavior? Probably from their families. Although adults don't typically spend as much time playing video games as kids do, they watch a lot of television. Just like video games, TV is a way to take a mental break and escape reality. An escape is certainly fine in moderation, but the average five hours and eleven minutes Americans watch TV each day is inarguably cutting into time that would be better spent in other ways.[2] It might not always feel like a huge waste of time in an average day, but considering how that time adds up to an average of nine years over the course of a lifetime, it's easy to see how TV is one of our most time-consuming minors. If you still aren't convinced to turn off the TV, consider this fact. When TV watching is broken down by economic class, only 33 percent of the wealthy watch more than one hour of TV each day, compared to 77 percent of the poor.[3] While there are a lot of factors that contribute to this statistic, I have to wonder if people who have become wealthy weren't big TV watchers to start with and instead focused more of their time on meaningful outcomes.

Watching TV not only engages us in a minor activity in the moment, but also provides fuel for further distraction. American children watch about sixteen thousand TV commercials each year, which influence views on what is truly important in life from a young age.

While many minors are pleasurable, I want to point out that they aren't always activities people enjoy. Sometimes the minors can be doing household chores, running errands, or spending extra time doing something in a specific way. People find themselves focusing on a multitude of tasks like this, and pretty soon, they wonder where their day went. Instead of running across town to pick up that specific item, maybe that hour could have been better spent working toward achieving long-term goals.

There are also some minor activities that mask themselves as majors by seeming as if they were healthy and positive—spending countless hours reading self-help books or going to educational seminars, for example. If one fails to apply what is learned, these majors become minors, or distractions. In my mind, this is even worse than many other vices, because people gain a clear idea of what they need to be doing to help themselves, but they don't ever apply it.

With all of the minors we face today, it's no wonder they can derail our progress. Luckily, the next section will shed some light on the best way to avoid the minors and focus on what's more important.

Transitioning to the Majors

Going from the minors to the majors is, as the name implies, a major life change. It takes planning, discipline, and hard work. Instead of giving in to urges that strike you in the moment, you have to think about the big picture. The good news is that while transitioning to the majors requires work, it will also help you maximize your efforts and conserve energy, because you'll be cutting back on tasks that aren't a good use of your time.

In order to start focusing on the majors, it is important to develop a clear vision for your goals. The following section breaks down each of the majors that lays the foundation for an abundant life. Regardless of your personal or professional goals, current occupation, or age, these areas of life can make or break a person's happiness and success. If you spend time and effort every day thinking about and working on the majors, your life will change for the better.

This section will give you the opportunity to reflect on these parts of your current life and how they compare to the ideal day you designed in the first chapter.

Health

Have you ever noticed that people often sacrifice their health to make money, then sacrifice their money to try to improve their health? It isn't a smart strategy. Our health needs to be a top priority in our lives. Health is more than just being alive; it's about the quality of life that you enjoy while you're here. Poor health can limit which activities you can participate in, where you can travel, and what you can eat, and as a result, it affects your ability to live your ideal day.

I want to point out that being in good health isn't about what "shape" you're in. The media like to describe our bodies as pears, apples, twigs, hourglasses, and who knows what else, but a person's shape isn't the way to assess his or her health. Often, people whom the media would consider to be in perfect "shape" actually have below-average health and energy. Some people stay thin no matter what they eat, so their physical appearance doesn't pay the price for their poor choices. Fried foods still cause high cholesterol in thin people. The lack of vitamins, nutrients, or enough sleep weakens the immune system in people of all shapes, leaving them more susceptible to colds, the flu, and a myriad of other sicknesses. Just because people are thin doesn't mean they are healthy.

On the flip side, there are many people in this world who don't fit the media's image of the ideal body shape, but they have an abundance of energy. The first thing in the morning, they come flying out of bed excited to be alive! They go and go all day long, making progress and accomplishing goals in all aspects of their lives. When they come home at night, they have a surplus of energy left over and have to turn it off mentally and emotionally to get to sleep. However, most people wouldn't peg them as the picture of good health, because their body mass index is on the higher end of the spectrum.

I was living in Pasadena, California, a few years ago, and my roommate was a male fitness model who appeared on magazine covers. He didn't have a six-pack; he had an eight-pack. His arms bulged in an intimidating yet aesthetically pleasing way. This guy worked out and sculpted his body every single day, and he did one heck of an amazing job. On the outside, he was the image of peak fitness.

Unfortunately, his health was another story. At the time, he was taking fat-burning pills, muscle enhancers, and who knows what else. These supplements were destroying his body on the inside, even though his outside shape was ideal, according to society's standards. A few years after living like this, he eventually burned out his adrenal glands. Doctors told him that he was dangerously close to death. He was put on long-term bed rest until his body could recuperate. He was able to make a full recovery, and he now takes a different approach to staying healthy.

Good health doesn't mean achieving a specific weight, clothing size, or the perfect abs; health is all about the amount of energy you have.

REFLECTION

On a scale from 0 to 10 (0 being absolutely no energy and 10 being an abundance of energy, day in and day out), where would you rate your current level of health and energy?

I'm sure there are some of you thinking, "Getting a 10 is not possible. A 10 would be perfect and no one is perfect; therefore the best I could ever be is 9.9." That's fine. We all think about this type of thing differently. If you find yourself in this situation, rate yourself from 0 to 9.9.

How does this rating compare to the health you imagined for yourself in your Ideal Day vision?

LIVE IT CHALLENGE

What if I told you there was a quick and easy fix that would greatly improve your health? This magic pill would decrease your chance of getting lung cancer by 30 percent, type 2 diabetes by 50 percent, breast cancer (in women) by 25 percent, as well as strengthen your heart and bone density. Actually, this magic pill would drastically cut your chances of dying by numerous diseases. Would you take this pill?

The pill doesn't exist, at least not in pill form. However, the quick and easy fix is a real thing! Better yet, it's free and doesn't have any dangerous side effects. The answer? Walking. Numerous studies have generated the aforementioned findings, and participants typically walked up to three hours per week, breaking their exercise into shorter increments, such as thirty minutes per day.[4]

Another benefit to walking regularly is the "exercise" it gives your brain. Light exercise from walking stimulates production of brain-derived neurotropic factor, a molecule that nurtures the creation of new neurons and synapses that underlie learning.[5]

Walking is something so simple, yet many of us do not do it enough. Make it a goal to walk more often than you currently do. Keep a walking journal if you must or put a reminder alert in your calendar.

Emotional Intelligence

Do you live a life of action or reaction? Do you choose how you are feeling no matter what is going on around you, or do you constantly spend time reacting to whatever life places in front of you? We have all experienced how unpredictable life is and how hard it can be to stay positive when things don't go as well as we had hoped. Even though it's sometimes hard to control our emotions, it is crucial to work at it. When we can control our emotions instead of letting them control us, we have high emotional intelligence.

The following is an example of how two people can go through the same situation but react totally differently, based on emotional intelligence.

SCENARIO	TRACY	JESS
Wakes up in the morning and gets ready for work.	Feels OK.	Feels OK.
Accidentally spills coffee on clothes during the ride to work.	Thinks the morning has taken a turn for the worse. Gets tense and frustrated.	Isn't fazed by the stain. It's just clothes.
Realizes important documents are still at home on the kitchen table.	Wonders if the day can get any worse.	Recognizes this isn't an ideal situation, but it's OK because everyone makes mistakes. Focuses on how to be productive without the documents.
Gets ready for a meeting at noon and feels excited, looking forward to it as a highlight of the day. Ten minutes before the meeting, the other person cancels.	Realizes the day can get worse and wonders what other terrible things are in store.	Immediately thinks about how else to use this time to be productive. Comes up with a few options and uses that hour to do some research on a new project.
Returns home at the end of the day.	Feels bitter about this lousy day and can't seem to shake a bad mood. Turns to something that will bring immediate happiness but won't help in the long run, like junk food, shopping, or video games.	Thinks about what an extraordinary day it was! Feels good about going with the flow and wonders what else could be accomplished that evening.

Now here is what's interesting: both Tracy and Jess had similar experiences, but based on the parts of that day they chose to focus on, the meaning they chose to give what happened, and the actions they took, they got vastly different results and felt differently about themselves and their day. Jess kept an eye on what was really important, instead of fixating on minor frustrations.

It isn't fun to be in a bad mood, but negative emotions also take a serious toll on physical health. Thanks to a powerful mind-body connection, stress and negative emotions can manifest into physical symptoms like headaches, stomach ulcers, high blood pressure, sexual problems, and sleep loss.

Poor emotional health can also weaken your body's immune system, making you more likely to get colds and other infections during emotionally difficult times. To make matters worse, when people are feeling stressed, anxious, or upset, they may not take care of their health as well as they should. It can be easier to eat unhealthy fast food instead of cooking, and it takes less energy to watch TV than it does to go to the gym. Abuse of alcohol, tobacco, or other drugs may also be a sign of poor emotional health.

On the flip side, positive emotions can have a beneficial impact on your health. Laughter can even help cure disease. A great example of this is how journalist and world peace advocate Norman Cousins credited laughter for helping cure a serious and painful type of arthritis. He worked with his physician to control his laughter so that he could use it as an alternate form of therapy. Cousins would make himself laugh for ten minutes straight, which he said would produce an anesthetic effect and give him at least two hours of pain-free sleep. He continued this regimen, along with high doses of vitamin C and a mental focus on love, hope, and positivity. Although his chances of being cured of his disease were estimated at around one in five hundred, Cousins beat the odds.[6]

REFLECTION

On a scale from 0 to 10 (0 being nowhere close to where you want to be and 10 being exactly where you want to be), where would you rate yourself in the area of emotional intelligence?

How does this compare to the health you imagined for yourself in your Ideal Day vision?

LIVE IT CHALLENGE

When something doesn't go as well as you hoped, here are three questions you can ask yourself to help build your emotional intelligence:

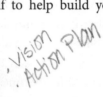

1. What is great about this?

2. What can I learn from this?

3. What can I do better next time?

As you answer all three questions, use them (especially number three) to help you create an action plan toward making progress. Action is always better than intention.

Laughter Challenge

I've heard that people laugh less as they get older. Challenge yourself to watch or participate in something daily that helps you stay laughing for at least ten minutes.

Intimate Relationships

This can be one of the most rewarding areas of human life. We are hardwired to seek out a partner to share in our greatest triumphs, support us in our darkest days, and offer companionship everywhere in between. Even when other aspects of life are going well, when people lack this type of relationship, everything else can seem meaningless.

The key to lasting and positive intimate relationships is focusing on giving, rather than receiving. Far too often, people think a relationship is a place you go to get something—a cure for loneliness or a quick fix for happiness. The truth is, you have to be happy with yourself before entering a relationship. Another person can't magically fill the void that develops when you don't love yourself on your own. That is not what relationships are made for; a relationship is a place you go to *give*.

If you want a relationship to last, an effective way to do it is to define the greatest gifts you want to share and go out and find a person who needs and wants those gifts. The greatest gifts you possess can be anything, as long as they are a reflection of your true self. For example, some people are born nurturers. They find purpose in nurturing others, and their partner will naturally be a recipient of this gift. Other people have an indelible sense of humor that is a gift to everyone around them, especially their significant other. Some people are musicians and share their emotions and affection through music.

Take time to think about your personality and talents, and create a list of a couple of things you are great at because they come so naturally to you. Some of these gifts will be things you already know you love doing, and others might be aspects of your personality that other people love about you. If you aren't sure, ask a close friend or family member—sometimes other people can offer a new perspective you hadn't considered. Whatever you identify as your greatest gifts, the best match for you is someone who appreciates those gifts and who can reciprocate with gifts you appreciate as well.

If you are already in a relationship, thinking about and discussing your own gifts and your partner's gifts can help strengthen or renew your relationship.

REFLECTION

On a scale from 0 to 10 (0 being nowhere close to where you want to be and 10 being exactly where you want to be), where would you rate yourself in the area of intimate relationships?

How does this compare to the intimate relationship you imagined in your Ideal Day vision?

LIVE IT CHALLENGE

If you are currently in an intimate relationship:

- What are the parts of you that you want to share most with the person closest to you?

- How will you let that person know how important it is to you to be able to share these gifts?

- What is your plan to better share your gifts?

If you are not currently in an intimate relationship:

- Sometimes a part of your personality can feel repressed if you aren't sharing your gifts with anyone. Even though you aren't currently in a relationship, think about how you could share your gifts with others. How could your friends, family, or community benefit from you sharing your gifts?

CHAPTER 3:

FOCUSING ON THE MAJORS

PART 2

Let's consider some more majors, including family, finances, and your professional life.

Family

Many people nowadays are so focused on achieving professional goals and keeping up with the daily grind that family often gets left on the back burner. This is especially true in parts of the world that have transformed into modern metropolises where commerce is king. In societies where there is enormous pressure to make work the top priority, it's important to take a step back and realize that the most valuable things in life are people. Whether it's your parents, children, siblings, cousins, or friends whom you consider to be a part of your family, make sure you take enough time to nurture those relationships.

I'm sure this advice doesn't come as a surprise. We all know we *should* be spending more time focusing on family, but our actions don't always match up. Unfortunately, the perfect time to concentrate on family rarely arrives, because life is busy. Things always come up. Instead of waiting for the time, you have to *make* the time.

You may be thinking, "I know my family, and they don't really *get* me or understand me like my friends do." I hear you. This isn't an attempt to get you to rekindle relationships you have already found to be unhealthy or unfulfilling. You need a network that *feels* like family, whether these people are actually related to you or not. They are your support system, and they will offer you love, appreciation, and understanding. You need people you can count on to be there when life knocks you down. Relationships like these deserve nurture and attention, and they won't thrive on autopilot.

I went to see a Garth Brooks concert in Las Vegas in 2012.[1] Brooks had been semiretired from the music scene for a few years, but now he was performing again, and longtime fans were eager to see him. During the concert, he talked about his background and experience in the music industry. His career began very humbly, with him putting in a lot of time without getting any traction. He stayed focused and didn't give up. Finally, after years of hard work, he started gaining momentum, booking bigger gigs, and becoming known in country music. That's when his career took off, his songs topped the charts, and he went from being an undiscovered singer to a household name. He was suddenly living his dream.

His personal life, however, was another story. Being a famous singer is an extremely demanding job. Tours and appearances eat up a great deal of time, forcing relationships with family members to the back burner. Even though he was living the professional life of his dreams, he was missing his kids growing up. He decided that family was more important to him than propelling his career forward, so he put his music on hold to be a full-time father and husband. He didn't know if his fans would still be there when he came back, but it was a chance he was willing to take.

What a beautiful act of courage for him to make a change that went against what other people wanted from him and put his own needs and his family's needs first.

The best option for you probably isn't quitting your job, unless you have a great deal of money saved up and can ensure the financial well-being of your family for many years to come. However, there are other things you could do to start making your family a higher priority. You never know how long you will be blessed to have these people in your life.

REFLECTION

On a scale from 0 to 10 (0 being nowhere close to where you want to be and 10 being exactly where you want to be), where would you rate your relationships with the people you care about most—your family members, whether biological or honorary?

How does this compare to the relationships with family you imagined for yourself in your Ideal Day vision?

LIVE IT CHALLENGE

What can you do right now to start inching your way toward that vision? Here are a few places to start:

- Shut it off and be present. Technology has done wonders for improving our quality of life, but too much time switched on can take away from building relationships. Instead of having conversations, kids are playing games, adults are checking work e-mail, and everyone is distracted by social media. Make it a point to set aside time regularly where everything is turned off and you spend time just being present with the people you love. Set a timer if you have to. Just don't use the one on your cell phone!

- Schedule a family night each week to do something fun together. Let everyone take turns choosing activities or what to eat for dinner.

- If your job offers flexible scheduling, use it to spend more time with your family. If your job doesn't offer it, consider talking to your manager or human resources leader about having this as a benefit. Many companies are now allowing employees to work from home on certain shifts or take a couple of hours off at a time to attend to family needs.

Professional Life

Several years ago, I spent a few months living in a rural farming village in Uganda as a volunteer through Students Partnership Worldwide. When I arrived, the nongovernmental organization field coordinators took me to where I would be staying for the duration of my trip. My bedroom was inside of an old, broken-down schoolhouse. There was no electricity, no running water, and no toilets. The building had no doors, and the windows had old, broken, and bent rusted bars on them. To help me keep my belongings safe each day when I was out teaching organic farming, a lockable door had been placed in a small room in the back corner of the building. Despite the living conditions, it was one of the most beautiful places I had ever been in my entire life.

Every single morning, I timed it just right so that I could wake up and watch the sunrise. I would push open the big metal shutters, lean out the window a little, and watch the colors unfold—orange, red, and even purple as the sun peeked up over the pineapple fields.

About a hundred feet outside of my bedroom window there was the tiny village clinic. It was not a hospital; just a small clinic. Each morning as I was waking up and watching the sunrise, I'd see a little old man come out of the clinic with his long thatch broom, slowly inching his way down a long dirt path, sweeping leaves in a rhythmic motion: sweep-sweep, step-step, sweep-sweep, step-step. He did this all the way to the main road. Then he would turn around and do it again all the way back to the front door of the clinic: sweep-sweep, step-step, sweep-sweep, step-step. When he was finished, the look on his face showed pride, satisfaction, and certainty that the task he just completed mattered. It was the look you see on a person's face when they are doing what they were put on this planet to do.

Every morning, as I watched the little old man sweep, I got more curious. After all, he was sweeping dirt. How much difference can a little sweeping possibly make on a dirt path? What was crazy was that this man never missed. He was up sweeping every day exactly at sunrise. After two and a half months of watching him sweep each morning, I couldn't handle my curiosity anymore.

I didn't speak his language, so I found a local friend who did and asked her to help me interview him. We walked over and approached this man, and she asked him, "Sir, why do you sweep the leaves each day?" He shrugged his shoulders, and the look on his face made it seem as if he had been asked an odd question. He responded to her and she translated, "Because I am supposed to."

Now let me warn you, if you have ever traveled overseas with an American, you know that we are often guilty of believing that if someone did not understand us, we must not have been speaking loudly enough. So as silly as it was, I turned back to them and tried to clarify my question in a voice that was near yelling: "No, *why* are you sweeping the leaves?"

The old man looked at me with confusion, and my friend shook her head and rolled her eyes at me. My communication skills seemed to have embarrassed her. She turned to the old man again, thought for a second, and worded the question in a different way. All of a sudden, the old man grinned from ear to ear and his eyes filled with light and passion. I knew he understood my question before he said anything else.

"That's it!" I exclaimed, grabbing my friend, who was mentally deleting one of my cool points every moment.

The old man shared his story, my friend took a moment to digest the information, and then she translated, "The *reason* I sweep the leaves is that I believe every human being, whether it be a small baby about to enter this world or a sick or elderly person about to leave this world, deserves a clear path to do so."

I was awestruck. My jaw might have hit the ground. I was standing in the presence of a man who did something seemingly simple each day, but through deep purpose and meaning, it became a profound action. It made me think hard about what it means to have a fulfilling job—a mission that you carry out through work. Clearly, there is more than what meets the eye.

When I speak in front of audiences, I ask them to make a noise to represent how they feel about these terms: *job*, *career*, and *mission*. *Job* gets a few whimpers, *career* gets some cheers, but *mission* (*purpose* or *passion*) gets stand-up-on-your-chair whoops and hollers. When it comes to your professional life, my best advice is to find a deeper meaning in what you do. It can be complex or simple; just make sure it is significant to you. By focusing on this meaning you create, you will find yourself more motivated to keep going.

If you have tried to find passion and purpose in your current work situation but simply cannot do it, maybe it's time for a change.

REFLECTION

Which area are you currently spending the majority of your time in each day—a job, a career, or living your mission and purpose in life?

Once you know what category you are in, give it a rating from 0 to 10.

How does this compare to the professional life you envisioned for yourself in your Ideal Day vision?

LIVE IT CHALLENGE

In your professional life, are you living your mission, purpose, and passion? If you aren't there yet, are you at least on the right career path for having a fulfilling and gratifying position? Sometimes people have to work their way up to build their ideal professional lives, but that doesn't mean you should wait until you arrive at that point to start feeling good about it. Brainstorm on how you could add even more meaning and purpose to what you're already doing. Are there small changes that would make a big impact, like learning new skills or strengthening relationships with coworkers? Take responsibility for your engagement level at work and make the changes that will make you happier.

If you aren't on track for living your mission, purpose, and passion, use the following three steps to identify the types of positions that would allow you to thrive:

1. Using the same concept of thinking about our greatest gifts for the intimate relationships category, let's translate this to the professional world. Take out a pen and paper and make a list of your natural gifts and talents. No matter how simple or complex they are, write them down.

2. Next, circle the top five gifts or talents that you feel are most important—the ones you want to share the most.

3. Finally, make a list of all the ways you are aware of that allow those gifts and talents to shine. For example, if you have been blessed with giving, loving, nurturing, listening, and caring as your gifts, careers that bring these gifts to the world include counseling, social work, mentoring, coaching, and being a psychologist or a therapist. The list doesn't stop there. There are a lot of ways to share these gifts with the world. When you determine the type of job that is a good fit for your greatest gifts and talents, your job or career can become your mission and passion.

Finances

There are many ways to make a good living and support yourself and your family, but finding an option that makes you 100 percent satisfied is a difficult thing and often a long journey. Many people sacrifice either their happiness at work or extra free time for a job that pays well, or their earning potential for a job they love. It is important to find a balance that works for you when it comes to making money and doing something you find interesting and rewarding. This is key for maintaining the motivation to work hard over the years.

Whether you earn a large or small salary, spending less and saving more will help you accumulate more financial wealth. It may seem like saving pennies will never amount to anything, but that is definitely not the case. For people who are willing to work hard, it has become easier over the years to grow up without much money and amass a fortune during a lifetime.

Thelma Pearl Howard was born into a poor farming family in Idaho in 1915, but she died a multimillionaire.[2] As a young adult, she enrolled in college but had to drop out because she couldn't afford the tuition. To make a living, she was working three different jobs, cleaning houses, working at a soda fountain, and doing part-time secretarial work, when she landed a job that would change her life's course—being a live-in housekeeper for Walt Disney's family.

While it may sound like Howard had it made from the time she got this position in 1951, Disney was actually a much smaller company at the time. Howard earned a modest salary, which was a little higher than the average for a housekeeper, but she recognized the opportunity. However, the job didn't come without challenges. The Disney family had been having a difficult time retaining a housekeeper. The housekeeper before Howard had been terminated because she didn't get along with the children. It seemed that keeping her position could prove to be a difficult task in itself, but Howard dedicated herself fully to the job and earned the love and respect of the Disney family.

As thanks for the great work she was doing, Walt Disney gave Howard shares of stock as a bonus every year for Christmas and her birthday. In the beginning, it wasn't worth much, but Howard never sold it, out of gratitude and respect for her boss. As Disney grew in popularity over the years, so did the value of the stocks and the quantity of shares Howard owned. As her wealth grew, her standards of living stayed the same, and she continued working through her late sixties.

When she passed away years later, a small group of her friends and family were called together for the reading of her will. They were shocked to learn her share of Disney stocks was worth $9.5 million. Howard left half to her developmentally disabled son and half to establish and operate a charitable foundation. She chose to live a humble lifestyle, knowing the money she saved would help people years after she was gone.

While having money to buy nice things can be desirable, the most attractive benefit of financial wealth is the ability to buy freedom in other areas of your life. Financial wealth enables you to do the things you want to do and gives you the free time to do them. The ideal situation is to transition from trading your time for money to having your money make money for you.

REFLECTION

In your current financial situation, from 0 to 10, where are you compared to where you want to be?

At that level, from 0 to 10, where are you compared to where you want to be?

How does this compare to the financial vision you imagined for yourself in your Ideal Day vision?

LIVE IT CHALLENGE

Based on where you currently are right now, what are your plans for making progress financially in your life? If you haven't created a personal budget already, take the time to do so. You should have a good understanding of how much you make each month, how much you need to cover necessary expenses and how much you have left over to save and invest.

Spirituality

As human beings, we yearn for a deeper understanding of our purpose in this world. Why are we here and what are we meant to learn and do? Spirituality is something that helps a lot of people make sense of the world around them and keeps them going when they face adversity.

Today, Nick Vujicic travels around the world inspiring people to find their purpose, especially in difficult times.[3] No stranger to adversity, Vujicic has tetra-amelia syndrome, a rare disorder that caused him to be born without arms or legs. He suffered from depression and loneliness as a child because of his physical condition. Vujicic's family is religious and his father worked as a pastor in their hometown, but Vujicic questioned God, both doubting his existence and wondering whether his condition was God's way of punishing him. As Vujicic became an adult, he began to find purpose in his life. He realized that if he could learn to be happy with the absence of limbs, he could inspire others to have strength, experience happiness and find their purpose in life as well.

When he was nineteen, Vujicic started speaking to audiences and sharing his story, which had an incredible impact on people. Years later, he was invited to speak at several university campuses in China, where suicide had become prevalent.[4] Top students were ending their lives because they were afraid of their future after graduation and not being able to find a good job. Vujicic was able to relate to students, whether they believed in the same God or a different one, and inspire them to have faith in their life's purpose. The suicide rate dropped immediately after Vujicic's outreach, and as a result he was invited back to connect with even more people through a nationally televised government show in China. As the word spread, he was invited to speak in Vietnam, Brazil, and many other countries around the world. People fill stadiums to see him speak, and governments invite him to speak on TV shows that are broadcast to entire nations. Vujicic credits his faith in God for becoming the happy person he is today and being able to inspire the people around him.

Now, I am not here to preach or tell you what you should or should not believe when it comes to spirituality. I am here to ask you this: Do you practice what you believe you should be doing in this category of your life? I can easily tell you that if you do not practice what you believe, this area of your life will always feel at least a little empty.

REFLECTION

From 0 to 10, how would you rate your spiritual life? A 0 would be knowing what you believe in but not following it, whereas a 10 would be wholeheartedly following your beliefs in all that you do.

How does this compare to the spiritual life you imagined for yourself in your Ideal Day vision?

LIVE IT CHALLENGE

Do you practice what you believe in to the fullest? For example, if you believe in going to church, temple, or another organized worship service, are you actually getting yourself there? If you believe helping others is a fundamental part of your spirituality, are you taking action to help others or simply thinking about it?

Take a step to transform your intentions into actions.

Summary

I highly recommend you revisit this chapter once a month and use this system to rerate where you are in each major area of life. This will help you build the habit of continually assessing and reassessing your progress. It's also encouraging to see your scores improve as a direct result of your diligence and hard work.

In the next chapter, we will uncover how to bridge the gap between how you currently rate your life in the majors and how you would rate your dream life.

CHAPTER 4:

IGNITING YOUR EMOTIONAL ROCKET FUEL FOR RESULTS

Every person you meet in life is either a warning or an example—a warning of what not to do or an example of what to do. Which are you being right now in your life?

There is an enormous difference between *knowing what to do* and *doing what you know*. Something that I touch on in my speaking engagements with all of my audiences is *motivation*, and how to translate it into action. It seems that people almost always know what to do, but sometimes come up short on consistently following through with action. It's an interesting predicament, since it seems as if knowledge would be enough to get the ball rolling toward taking action.

Unfortunately, that isn't always the case.

This gap between knowing what to do and actually doing what you know holds true in all of the majors in life. Most people have enough knowledge about nutrition to be capable of making healthy eating choices, for example, but that doesn't mean they will. When people have the knowledge they need to improve their health, relationships, careers, finances, or anything else, but they choose not to take consistent daily action, they will never get the results they desire. This is true across the board.

Action is what separates top salespeople from those who are barely making it.

Action is the difference between having close relationships with friends and family, or losing touch.

Action is how some people stay fit and keep their mobility long after they are considered elderly, while others start to have trouble getting around at a much younger age.

Since taking effective and empowering action seems like the cure-all for living a better life, why is it such a hard thing for people to do? The reason is simple: they lack Emotional Rocket Fuel. Emotional Rocket Fuel is the source of strong motivation and the reason why people reach and exceed their goals. On your journey to living your ideal life, having Emotional Rocket Fuel is nonnegotiable. In fact, it is the single greatest influence on your life experience—whether you will meet your goals and how long it will take you to get there. Some people may be born with more intrinsic motivation than others, but luckily, it's something all of us can work to improve upon over time. This chapter focuses on how to discover and ignite the Emotional Rocket Fuel that will empower you to achieve rapid results in your life and business.

There are two key factors for building your Emotional Rocket Fuel each day:

1. Finding your Big Why

2. Activating your Big Why

Key #1 for Igniting Emotional Rocket Fuel— Finding Your Big Why

Your Big Why is your reason and purpose behind why you do what you do. It is the driving force that propels you forward and encourages you to keep going when you face adversity. When you falter and the thought of quitting crosses your mind, remembering your Big Why will give you the emotional fortitude you need to achieve the results you're after.

Most people struggle to define their Big Why, yet they don't realize that many times it is right in front of them. Some people work so their children can have a better future, some work to prove to others (or themselves) what they are made of, and some work so they don't starve. There are a myriad of sources of motivation, but often, people can get so caught up in their day-to-day activities that they lose a clear perspective on why they do what they do. Without this perspective, they go through the motions with their head down, lacking passion and a sense of purpose. Going through the motions is what you want to avoid! Think back to your ideal day. Was there ever a point where you envisioned yourself going through the motions of that day without being present? Didn't think so. You shouldn't do it in your real life either. Discovering and defining your Big Why and keeping it in mind will help fill your life with purpose and direction.

Some of the most powerful Big Whys are the ones where people work for a cause bigger than just themselves. One of my favorite examples of this comes from Rick and Dick Hoyt, better known as Team Hoyt.[1] Rick was born to Dick and Judy Hoyt in 1962. Until Judy went into labor, everyone expected a normal birth and a healthy baby. However, Rick was born with cerebral palsy, and complications at birth also left him a spastic quadriplegic. Doctors said there was no chance of Rick recovering, which made the possibility of living a "normal" life slim to none. They told Dick and Judy to institutionalize Rick, thinking it would be easier for them and make no difference to Rick. Dick and Judy didn't even consider this advice; their Emotional Rocket Fuel was ignited for making Rick's life as normal as possible.

Unlike other children, Rick couldn't speak or walk, but it was clear he understood the world around him. This made Dick and Judy fight even harder for Rick's inclusion in the public school system and the community. When Rick was ten, his family was able to get an interactive computer made that would allow him to communicate. The computer had a cursor that could highlight letters of the alphabet. Rick was able to select letters by tapping his head gently against a headpiece that was connected to his wheelchair. He surprised everyone by using the new computer to say, "Go Bruins!" (At the time, the Boston Bruins were contenders for the Stanley Cup. While this was exciting, friends and family laughed about Rick using his first words to cheer on the local hockey team, instead of taking the opportunity to officially say hello to them.)

Five years later and still using the computer to communicate, Rick told his dad that he wanted to participate in an upcoming race. A lacrosse player had recently been in an accident that left him paralyzed, and the community was having a five-mile benefit run. Dick wasn't a runner at the time, and five miles seemed like a long distance, but he agreed to run while pushing Rick in his wheelchair. They finished the race together, coming in next to last. For Rick, the race was life-changing. That night, he told Dick, "Dad, when I'm running, it feels like I'm not handicapped."

Suddenly, Dick was hit with an even Bigger Why. He would have never chosen to run races on his own, but knowing how it made his son feel, he was motivated to start seeking out races they could participate in together. Running took on a deeper and more powerful meaning, and it gave him the strength to get through the physical challenge, which was one he wasn't initially drawn toward.

Dick soon realized he could do more than just run while he pushed Rick in a wheelchair; he could get special equipment that would allow them to do triathlons together so they could race more often. They got a bicycle with a special second seat, and a boat for Rick to sit in while Dick swam and pulled him with a bungee cord. They didn't stop there. Dick kept training and was able to complete numerous Ironman competitions with Rick at his side. Over the years, they have participated in more than one thousand races of various distances, including seventy marathons. Adding to their list of achievements, Team Hoyt biked and ran across the United States in 1992, completing a full 3,735 miles in forty-five days. This is a remarkable accomplishment for a person who previously had no interest in competitive races. Dick's Big Why made all the difference. Instead of focusing on each grueling step, he kept his focus on the meaning behind his actions.

Imagine what would be possible in your life and business if you were able to use this same process in your health, relationships, or any of the major categories of life. If you work in sales, for example, and use this process, it will be the difference between taking a handful of actions each day hoping for positive results and actually having the Emotional Rocket Fuel to take the consistent actions necessary to get the results you are after.

My father was able to identify his Big Why when he found out he was going to be a dad. He went through a lot of financial hardships as a child, and he decided he never wanted his own children to go through that. The year I was born, he was able to take his sales from $38,000 per year to well over a million dollars the following year, all because he was able to activate his Emotional Rocket Fuel!

Your Big Why will help you with all of the major areas of your life. It will be the key ingredient to following through with the habits and rituals needed to build a happy and long-lasting intimate relationship. Your Big Why will also help you make better choices to positively impact your health, like eating better and getting exercise.

LIVE IT CHALLENGE

Thinking back to your Ideal Day vision, you highlighted numerous people, places, things, and emotions to include. Why are these elements important to you? Some reasons may come to mind right away, while others might be more complicated. Your challenge is getting to the root of why you envisioned your ideal day the way you did. When you can figure that out, you will uncover your Big Why and ignite your Emotional Rocket Fuel to help propel you toward extraordinary results in any (and every) major category of life.

- Brainstorm on your Big Why in both your personal and professional life.

- Once you have identified your Big Why, take the time to think about it each day. Keeping it in mind will help motivate you and keep you on track.

- Consider creating a visual reminder of your Big Why. Maybe it's a photo of your kids inside your wallet or a few inspirational words on a sticky note at your desk.

Imagine what you would be able to produce in all of the major areas of your life if you had the fuel to take the consistent daily actions that lead to the results you are after. The possibilities are endless!

Key #2 for Igniting Emotional Rocket Fuel— Activating Your Big Why

Once you've found your Big Why, you can't stop there. Knowing what motivates you is not enough to ignite consistent daily action in the long term. Activating your Big Why—turning thoughts into actions—requires some heavy mental lifting. There are a few different ways you can think about your situation that will help you cross the threshold of wanting something and not working toward it 100 percent, to fighting for what you want as hard as you can, every single day. The following strategies will help you activate your Big Why immediately.

Emotional Stacking

Since human emotions are quite complex, people typically have mixed feelings about any given situation. We can see both the positives and negatives of most circumstances, even if we consider a situation to be either good or bad. When it comes to taking action in our lives, we automatically and often subconsciously weigh these positive and negative emotions and use them as a guide for the choices we make. We do this hundreds of times every single day; it's how we make decisions.

From the moment people wake up in the morning, they are stacking their positive and negative emotions against each other to see which weighs more. For example, let's say your alarm goes off at six thirty in the morning on a normal workday. You think about how good it would feel to hit the snooze button and fall back asleep within a few seconds. You also think about how much you dislike rushing in the morning, how stressed it makes you feel, and the extra approval you would get from your boss for being a little early. You weigh both the positive and negative emotions that would result from hitting the snooze button, and you make a choice about whether you should get up. When you make your choice, you cross the emotional threshold of stacking your emotions to the point where you decide to take action.

To activate your Emotional Rocket Fuel and Big Why, you need to stack your emotions so that you cross the emotional threshold for taking action every single day. Luckily, there is a strategy for doing this. There are two basic types of motivation:

- Desire to experience something pleasurable

- Desire to avoid something painful

All of our actions boil down to stacking our emotions toward or against these two types of motivation.

Emotional Stacking Exercise
Take out your notebook and pen to record your answers.

- Think about taking action toward your Big Why and identify all of the emotions you have that fit under wanting to avoid pain. Brainstorm everything you can think of that would cause you pain today, tomorrow, and in fifty years if you don't take action now. Write down the negative effects on your life and emotions.

- Next, think about taking action toward your Big Why and identify all of the emotions you have that fit under the desire to experience something pleasurable. Again, you want to think hard and come up with a complete list of everything that would cause you pleasure today, tomorrow, and in fifty years if you do start taking action now. Write down the positive effects on your life and emotions.

- You will use these lists as the basis for stacking your emotions.

Now that you have recorded the various motivations you have around taking action toward your Big Why, thinking logically, it's easy to see how these different factors could cause you to take action. The challenge lies in making the shift from a *cognitive* understanding to an *emotional* understanding. This is the difference between knowing what to do and actually doing it.

Take a look at how many points you listed under wanting to experience pleasure versus wanting to avoid pain. Some of these points are more powerful than others because of the types of emotions you naturally associate with them. Understanding how this works is essential for finding the right balance of motivational factors that will push you past the threshold for taking action.

Most people are naturally more motivated to avoid pain than pursue pleasure. We become accustomed to a certain quality of life, and downgrading to a lesser experience makes us uncomfortable. That's why any type of pain that threatens our quality of life can be especially motivating.

Going back to our alarm clock example, how quickly do you jump out of bed when you have an early morning meeting with your boss or an important client? Probably a lot quicker than you do on a normal workday. This is because you're thinking about how terrible it would be to run late, or worse, accidentally sleep through the meeting. The repercussions could cause you to lose credibility, damage your career, or maybe even get you fired. It could be seriously painful. You are highly motivated to avoid that experience, so you don't hit the snooze button—you get up. Focusing on the negative consequences of not taking action can be much more powerful than just focusing on the positives. Maybe you're excited to meet with your boss or your important client, but is it the excitement that drives you out of bed in the morning? More likely, it's the desire to avoid the consequences of running late. Depending on the nature of your Big Why and your unique perspective, there is a combination of motivations that will push you past your own personal threshold for taking action. Everyone is different, and there isn't a single answer that works across the board.

The key to igniting Emotional Rocket Fuel is finding the combination that works for *you*. This process requires a bit of self-discovery. If you just recently identified your Big Why, knowing how to best motivate yourself to take action is a learning process. Sometimes the factors that are most effective in getting us to cross the threshold and take action aren't what we originally assumed they would be, and we need to rewire our thinking a bit to stack our emotions in a different way.

Many people naturally focus on the positive outcomes they want from their Big Why, but often they make more progress when they shift their focus to include thoughts on the negative outcomes from not taking action. This seems counterintuitive, so I want to make sure you watch out for this when you stack your emotions.

If you find yourself not taking action because you tend to focus on pleasure, you might need to add in some thoughts on pain to use as your own personal leverage. If you're excited about taking action toward your Big Why, that's great. But is it enough to ignite the Emotional Rocket Fuel to keep you highly motivated every single day? Or will you feel like hitting the snooze button once in a while? Make yourself think about the painful outcomes that could result from not taking action, even if it's an unpleasant thought. For example, what are you going to miss out on by not taking action? What opportunities are you throwing out the window? How will you feel knowing you didn't reach your goals simply because you chose not to take action? These thoughts aren't as fun as focusing on the pleasant outcomes that could result from taking action, but they can certainly help motivate you and remind you of your Big Why. The key is to find the right balance of motivational factors for both pursuing pleasure and avoiding pain.

LIVE IT CHALLENGE

Refer back to the lists you created in the Emotional Stacking exercise.

Now that you understand how some motivations are more powerful than others, revisit how these factors make you feel. Instead of thinking logically about the reasons you should take action, let your emotions guide you. Which points bring out that fire in your belly for wanting to take action? When you identify a reason that strikes a chord in your heart, focus on that reason and feel the emotions behind it. Try this strategy with various points you wrote down, and take note of how effective they are at pushing you past the threshold for taking action. Once you are able to find a point that moves you emotionally, look for the next and "stack it" on top of the first. As you stack one on top of the other, you should feel your Emotional Rocket Fuel increase. Repeat this process until you find yourself unable to avoid action any longer and are driven to take action *now*. In the beginning, this is a learning process. Practice and see what types of thoughts give you the maximum amount of Emotional Rocket Fuel.

Now that you have identified how to stack your emotions, you need to focus on doing it every single day to stay motivated. On the journey to living your dream life, building this Emotional Rocket Fuel will help you keep pushing forward even when you encounter challenges along the way.

Overcoming Fears

One roadblock many people face when igniting their Emotional Rocket Fuel is the ability to manage their associations with fear. Sometimes taking the actions necessary to meet important goals is a scary process. It takes people out of their comfort zones, which can be a little unpleasant. However, many times that is an unavoidable part of making progress. If people do not take control of the associations they have with fear, they will limit their ability to take positive, life-changing actions. On the flip side, when people are able to control their fear and take action, they can provide themselves with even more Emotional Rocket Fuel, because taking action is an accomplishment in itself. No matter what happens in the end, displaying courage and bravery feels good.

Take a moment to think about a fear that has been holding you back from taking the actions necessary to get the results you want. Maybe the basis of your fear is rejection, or wasting time and ultimately failing. Or maybe you're afraid of how your life would change if you were successful. Whatever the fear, make sure you identify it now.

To stack weight emotionally against our fears, sometimes it helps to hear how other people have acted courageously when faced with fears even bigger than our own. You may have heard of Malala Yousafzai, a sixteen-year-old girl from Pakistan. She is known around the world for being a gender-equality education activist. Yousafzai's goal has been to not only get an education for herself but to stand up for what is right and help other girls get the education they deserve.[2]

Yousafzai grew up in an area where the Taliban were fighting for control of her neighborhood and its people. The Taliban made it clear they did not want girls and young women getting an education, and they threatened physical harm to anyone who defied their wishes. Inspired by her father, who is also an education activist, Yousafzai became a blogger for the BBC so she could share her story with the world. This was a particularly dangerous and courageous action for her to take, but she wanted to do it in the hopes of making a difference for other girls like her. When she first started blogging, she was writing under a pen name and speaking out against the Taliban softly so as not to stir up too much trouble. As her blog grew in popularity and she could see how her words were making an impact, her Big Why became even more solidified. She felt at her core that defying the Taliban and fighting for education equality was the right thing to do. Yousafzai also naturally used the emotional stacking process to weigh her options, and she decided the reward for speaking out was worth the risk and still better than following the Taliban's wishes. These factors kept her focused on her mission and purpose in life, even when she was afraid.

As Yousafzai's popularity began to grow, so did the Taliban's hatred toward her. In the summer of 2012, she received multiple death threats from the Taliban in an attempt to scare her and get her to stop speaking out. On October 9, 2012, as she was sitting in the back of the school bus on her way home from taking exams, her bus was stopped by a man. The students thought he looked like a journalist, so they weren't alarmed. He made his way to the back of the bus and asked which girl was Malala. She identified herself—the only girl who chose not to wear a head scarf. The man pulled out a gun and shot Yousafzai in the face. The bullet entered her head, went down her neck, and was later found in her shoulder. Miraculously, she survived. This bullet was neither the beginning nor the end of her fight for freedom and education for women and children around the world.

After being flown to England for multiple surgeries, Yousafzai was eventually able to go to school there. Although she was forced to leave her hometown because her actions made her an easily accessible target for the Taliban, she continues to speak about politics, freedom, and women's and children's rights, only now she has an even larger international platform to hear her message. She has written a book about her fight, and she perseveres in speaking up for what she believes is right.

Yousafzai is the perfect example of what can happen when you stack enough Emotional Rocket Fuel around your Big Why: it overpowers your fears. Yousafzai activated her Big Why and found the strength and courage to take consistent action to reach her goals, even when she was afraid. After considering Yousafzai's story, you can see how courage isn't the absence of fear; it's having fear and taking action in spite of it. A way to tap into that courage is by building your Emotional Rocket Fuel.

LIVE IT CHALLENGE

- What fears in your life currently slow you down or keep you from taking the action necessary to achieve the results you are after?

- How can you use those fears as your fuel for taking action, instead of allowing fear to control you?

- How can you remind yourself of this concept daily to help you keep moving forward and making progress?

The Hard-Easy versus the Easy-Hard

The second roadblock that can knock people off track when they are striving to achieve rapid results is choosing the easy-hard versus the hard-easy. The hard-easy is when people choose to do the hard stuff first, knowing that if they build the mental, emotional, and physical muscles now, everything else in the future will be much easier. On the flip side, the easy-hard is when people avoid all the hard stuff and focus on the easy stuff first, hoping that somehow they can get the results they desire without ever having to actually do the hard stuff.

In just about every major category of life, you are going to have some activities or tasks that are harder than others. If you choose to do the harder tasks first, you will be setting yourself up to win, rather than setting yourself up to struggle further down the road.

A great example of someone who was able to use this concept in his life and change history was Nelson Mandela. He consistently represented what I refer to as taking the hard-easy path. Mandela strongly believed in equality, which was a controversial viewpoint in apartheid South Africa, where racism had been institutionalized. He became a lawyer and stood strong against the apartheid government and helped push for progress even when faced with severe consequences. He was arrested numerous times throughout his career and continued to fight even at the threat of imprisonment.[3]

He had so much Emotional Rocket Fuel for bringing equality to the people of South Africa that he was not willing to lie down and allow things to unjustly stay the way they were. He refused to settle for the status quo, and he stood his ground and fought (nonviolently) for what was right. One of the most well-known periods of his life was when Mandela served more than twenty-seven years in prison, from 1962 to 1990, as a consequence of fighting for equality.

I remember the first time my father had the opportunity to meet with Mandela. My father was very excited to ask him how he was able to stay mentally strong and survive all those years in prison. When he asked Mandela this question, Mandela rose up, took a strong hold of my father's arm, looked straight into his eyes and exclaimed, "I did not survive. I prepared!"

The easy thing for Mandela to do in prison would have been to allow anger and frustration to build toward the people who put him there. If he would have chosen this route, he would have spent twenty-seven years allowing his emotions to consume him. We will never know what would have happened after his release if that were the case, but I can almost guarantee he would not have been able to end apartheid and become a leader who was celebrated around the globe.

Instead of allowing his frustrations to consume him, Mandela used his time to prepare. He studied the people who put him in prison, he learned to speak their language, and he did his best to prepare each day for his release. He worked toward better understanding, empathizing with those who imprisoned him and learning to find what he could respect about them. He did what was hard, so that his fight would be easier down the road.

Upon his release, he was able to become a leader in South Africa and partner with President F. W. de Klerk to help end apartheid. Later he became South Africa's first black president and a personified symbol around the world for peace. All this was possible because he chose to do the hard-easy path versus the easy-hard.

While Mandela's story is certainly courageous, you don't have to be caught in a controversial social or political situation to take the hard-easy path. Here are a few examples of how this concept applies to day-to-day life.

At the gym, the hard-easy is learning to fall in love with whatever you want to do the least. For example, many men spend all of their time on cardio and sculpting their upper bodies, dreading the day they have to focus on their legs. Instead, if they learned to fall in love with squats, everything else would be easy.

In business, the hard-easy would likely start with cold-calling or door-knocking. Many people love marketing, or even accounting (yes, some actually do love it), yet hate the grueling process of cold-calling. By starting with cold-calling (if that's the most dreaded task), the day is bound to get easier.

In finances, the hard-easy is spending less than you make and investing the difference. Now I am sure this does not sound like rocket science, but how many people do you know (maybe even yourself) who do not follow this simple principle? The hard-easy in this case would be to start saving like crazy and studying to learn all the different types of investments that are available. By slowly investing year after year, over time you might get to a point in your life where you no longer have to actually go to work anymore and your investments would pay for your lifestyle.

LIVE IT CHALLENGE

- What areas of your life are you choosing to do the easy-hard versus the hard-easy way? Think about all of the majors: health, emotional intelligence, intimate relationships, family, professional life, finances, and spirituality.

- Make a simple commitment to pick one of your major categories of life and start applying the hard-easy concept today. Start with one positive action at a time and build momentum to make hard-easy a way of life. You will be amazed at the results!

You now have the tools you need for creating the Emotional Rocket Fuel that will make the difference in reaching your goals. Remember, building and maintaining this motivation is something that takes dedication and practice. For the best results, you need to spend time working on it every day. The more you practice, the more you will improve and the easier it will become.

CHAPTER 5:

FALLING IN LOVE
WITH HARD WORK

The message our society gives to young people has changed a lot over the years. Instilling the value of hard work and long-term dedication has given way to the importance of following passions and dreams. As a result, many young people today grow up being told they are special and can do anything they want in life. We live in an age where happiness has become paramount. There isn't anything wrong with that, except when people often feel happy when they experience progress, as progress is a direct result of hard work. Instead of being prepared to do the hard work that will eventually lead to a fulfilling life, people think they can simply skip to the end results. If you're reading this book, you've already figured out that it doesn't exactly work that way. The "good life" is not something that is promised or guaranteed to anyone. It is something you work for and create through your ambition, focus, and determination.

Some of you are probably thinking, "Not another lecture on learning how to work hard!" I'm not trying to convince you to do hard work, but show you how to *fall in love* with hard work. Since there's no avoiding hard work on your path to success, why not try to enjoy it along the way? If you can learn to love hard work, you are much more likely to persevere through challenging times and ultimately reach your goals.

It's important to learn how to fall in love with the life that is directly in front of you and be happy in the here and now. Whether you're an exhausted single mother focused on raising your children, a struggling entrepreneur trying to maximize and monetize your business, or a coach doing your best to help your clients live their dreams, the information in this chapter is for you.

If you do not master the concept of falling in love with hard work, you're eventually going to run into the same problem you've run into your entire life. You probably know the feeling. That moment when what you are doing is no longer interesting, you've lost that spark in that guy or gal you're dating, or you just can't seem to get excited about the things that used to be so enjoyable. Next comes those grueling days contemplating if you should just give up, quit, and toss in the towel. It's like being in a prolonged state of limbo where you're unhappy where you are, but you can't seem to move forward. You don't want to start over from the beginning with something new, or stick it through and continue down the path and do what it takes to make it work.

Anyone can start a project, talk about how amazing his or her dreams are, or begin a relationship. It takes someone who is focused and determined, and who understands what true perseverance is all about, to finish that project and get the desired results. It takes courage and commitment to follow through on the promise you make when entering a marriage or long-term relationship. And it takes way more than you ever imagined in the beginning to turn your dream life into your actual life.

Harder Than Average

In the summer of 2004, I signed up for Semester at Sea's Voyage of Discovery, which is a floating university where you can take your classes while sailing around the world. I was sure this voyage would be the trip of a lifetime, and being able to go was an opportunity I couldn't resist. Since my dad was helping to fund my education, he wanted me to earn the privilege of going. We agreed that before going on the trip, I would learn what hard work is through personal experience. We made this agreement without defining the exact terms of how I would learn this lesson, so my first task was to go out and find hard work that I could do.

Although I was looking for "harder than average" work, my dad probably sensed I would settle on something that wasn't as challenging as he envisioned. To prevent that from happening, he suggested I spend the summer in Canada with my step-grandfather, whom I didn't know all that well. He gave me a bit of history on Grandpa, saying he started working at a lumberyard when he was young. Grandpa needed to earn a wage to support himself, so his first job was stacking lumber, a physically demanding but otherwise monotonous task. He proved to be a reliable and dedicated worker, so over time, he was able to move his way up to working as a manager, a foreman, a co-owner, and finally, the sole owner of the lumberyard. Eventually, Grandpa sold the business but remained friends with the people who bought it from him. Since he was still close with the current owners, he offered to help get me a spot on the team and send me to work. The lumberyard wouldn't pay me for my time, but if I did well, my dad would pay for my Semester at Sea program. I had no experience working with lumber, but I was open to the idea of having this be my lesson in hard work. After hearing Grandpa's story, I decided to go for it, since it sounded easy enough!

I'll never forget the day I arrived at my step-grandparents' house, and I don't think they will either. They brought me in and were excited for my new journey into manual labor, yet they were a little worried. Before my first day at work, they wanted to have a meeting to help me prepare and make sure I knew what I was getting myself into. My dad and uncle were also there for support.

Since it was the first meeting for my new job, I wanted to show up totally prepared. I ran downstairs, unpacked my suitcase, and grabbed my jeans, shoes, and work gloves. Then I thought to myself, "Shoot, it might rain. I better grab my rain jacket." On a whim, a cowboy hat and a CamelBak hydration pack seemed to make sense as well. You never knew when you might get thirsty— it was summer and warm outside.

I put all of this gear on for our meeting to show my grandparents I was prepared for this challenge. I ran back upstairs, walked into the living room, and my grandma burst into a fit of laughter that just about knocked her out of her chair. I didn't come across as prepared; instead, they now knew without a doubt that I wasn't knowledgeable or experienced in what I was about to be doing.

After their laughter subsided, they shared with me the daily schedule I would be following during my stay. I was expected to get myself to the side of a nearby freeway by six o'clock in the morning, so a man named Peter could pick me up in his van along with all of the other workers and drive us to the lumberyard. We would then stack lumber from seven in the morning to five in the afternoon and head back home. Although the transportation situation was a little out of the ordinary for me, the rest of it sounded pretty straightforward.

My grandparents said to make sure I had lots of rest, ate plenty of food, and stayed hydrated, because stacking lumber is really hard work. When they were finally satisfied with the myriad of warnings they gave me, I thanked them for their help, put my cowboy hat back on, and headed downstairs.

Before I made it to my bedroom, I overheard my uncle, dad, and grandparents making bets on how many days they thought I would last at this job. I stopped short and listened. They were laughing and saying I wouldn't last three days, let alone three months. They didn't think this kid from Southern California would be able to cut it doing hard manual labor.

That moment was a turning point for me. The Emotional Rocket Fuel to prove them wrong sprang up from out of nowhere. It coursed through my veins and became the driving force of my actions. I made the decision right then and there to prove a point—I was going to show my family that I was not only capable of surviving the hard work; I was going to thrive while doing it. I was going to show them I was mentally, emotionally, and physically stronger than they (or I) imagined.

In looking for a way to prove how strong and capable I was, I decided that doing the minimum and getting up at five thirty in the morning to get to the side of the freeway for work was not an option. Instead of following the daily schedule my grandparents had given me, I decided to take it up a notch. I would get up even earlier, at four thirty, and immediately go to the gym. I would lift weights and run for a half hour as my early morning workout. From there, I would eat breakfast, put my work clothes on, jump in the car, drive the twenty-five minutes to the side of the freeway, wait for Peter and the guys in the van, hop in, and drive an hour to the lumberyard. I would then stack lumber all day long with the team. From there, I'd jump back into the van with fourteen smelly guys and drive the two hours back to the car, thanks to rush-hour traffic. After that, I would drive twenty-five minutes back to the house and immediately go back to the gym for my evening workout. From there, I would eat dinner and go to bed, only to do it all over again the next day. I planned on doing this six days a week for three months.

In the beginning, I was full of steam, passion, and energy. I was ready to show everyone and myself what I was made of. I started off so strong—in the beginning.

My grandpa kept a close eye on me. Every morning, he would wake up and make sure I was up and still feeling OK. When I came home at night, he watched how I carried myself, making sure I wasn't getting injured from the heavy lifting. On the third day of watching me go to the gym before and after work, he warned me. He told me that he knew I was being ambitious and that I wanted to show them how hard I could work, but that I should be careful to avoid burning myself out. No way, I thought. I knew I was stronger and more capable than he imagined, and I was hell-bent on proving it.

The One Constant

Sure enough, a quarter of the way through my work agreement, I started to hate it. The desire to prove myself had worn off, and I began to notice some of the less desirable aspects of the job. Even though I was surrounded by coworkers, I felt lonely because none of them spoke English and we couldn't communicate. I would go the whole day without talking to anyone. At first, I didn't mind being alone with my thoughts, but after a few weeks, it got boring. Not only was the work itself monotonous but I wasn't stimulating my mind as my coworkers did through conversation. From lack of distraction, my head became clouded with negative thoughts. I started telling myself, "I'm better than this. I'm smarter than this. I'm more talented than this. I should be getting paid more than this." (I wasn't getting paid at all, but you get the point.) I questioned why I was wasting my time. I felt like quitting, leaving right then and there to do something better. Something I had been trained for or educated on, something where I could make more money or make more of a difference in the world.

I don't know if you've ever had this feeling about a job, but it can come out of nowhere, and man is it disappointing! When you first start at a new job, the beginning is so exciting. You are constantly learning new things and growing as a person. You are interested in getting to know your new coworkers. You can't wait to get to the office, knock out that project, and show people what you're made of. Your thoughts revolve around what a great opportunity you have in your new position. Somewhere along the way, you can get burned out and it can start to go sour.

This process often happens outside of work as well. You might be familiar with the feeling. It's when you're halfway through college and lose all desire to take more classes. It's when you're dating someone who once seemed like the most magical person on earth, but now he or she just seems like a friend you see all the time. It's when you're raising kids, and the little things they do go from exciting and cute to "Oh, that again?" (Often shown through how many photos people take of their first child versus their fourth.)

A lot of times when we lose excitement for things we once loved, we think our situation is changing, but really, it's our perspective that's changing. The newness wears off, and it becomes easier to see the less desirable aspects of an experience. After a few weeks at the lumberyard, nothing had changed, but I lost all excitement for being there. I was completely burned out, just like my grandpa had predicted. I weighed my options. I could give up, quit, and decide not to follow through on my word. I tried to tell myself it would be OK if I walked away from the situation. And I wanted nothing more than to just walk away!

At this point, I sat down and had a heart-to-heart conversation with myself. I had to make a decision. Although I wouldn't receive any terrible punishments if I quit, I knew I would lose my integrity. Since being known as a man of integrity is important to me, I thought hard about that compromise. Walking away from the job would cause immediate relief, but I would have to live with myself after making that decision. How long would it take me to feel good about myself after that, and how long would it take to rebuild my credibility with my family and friends who knew I had committed to this journey?

More importantly, if I couldn't find enjoyment in this job, why did I think I could find enjoyment doing something else? This realization was a turning point for me.

Most of the time when people get the "grass is greener" complex, they are forgetting one important factor—the one constant as you move through different situations is *you*! When you switch to a new job, a new city, or a new relationship, the single element that stays the same is *you*. If you are the type of person who is always looking for the next best thing, and you find it hard to be happy in the moment and enjoy what you have, that isn't going to change as your circumstances change.

Even if I quit my job stacking lumber, I could picture myself getting a different job that I would find frustrating in other ways. It was a revelation. My problem wasn't my job; it was *me*.

Instead of strategizing how I could get out of my current work commitment, I decided I should be brainstorming on how to fall in love with it. When a person is happy and loves the reality in front of them, everything else seems easy. No matter how hard the work is or how frustrating and exhausting it is, if you can learn to fall in love with where you're at right now, it gives you the ability to make everything else fun and enjoyable.

How do you know when you are in love? Love is when time disappears, you disappear, and nothing else matters. Love is that moment in life when you're in the zone and everything else flows around you. You might agree that all of this sounds great, but the problem is getting to this ideal state of mind. Falling in love with something you didn't originally enjoy is hard mental work. Just like doing heavy lifting at the gym, this task is an extreme workout for your mind and emotions.

The first step was making the decision to stick it through and stay at the lumberyard. I remember looking around and wondering how I could possibly start loving my job. Since I was going to continue stacking lumber for the foreseeable future, how could I transform it from a miserable experience to an enjoyable one? Considering how I felt at the time, it seemed impossible. However, I remembered back to the beginning of my time working there, and I did actually enjoy coming to work. My challenge would be to reignite that spark of enthusiasm. It was difficult, though, since I felt like I was in a different place emotionally than when I first started. I thought if I could figure out what specifically caused me to feel passionate in the beginning, I might be able to turn it into a formula and bring those emotions back to life.

Shift in Perspective

Thinking back to the first day on the job, the thrill was learning new skills and talents, and using my body in new ways. In doing this, I felt stronger and more capable, like I could kick some ass! That feeling of reward added even more Emotional Rocket Fuel, which lasted for a while, until it reached a plateau. To reignite that passion, I needed to find a way to continue learning while on the job and to continue building my mental, emotional, and physical strength.

In terms of learning more, unless my coworkers were up for letting me drive the forklift and operate the large wood-chopping and cutting machines, there wasn't much else for me to learn about lumber. But what if I could learn about other topics while I worked? I didn't have a lot of money at the time, but I took every penny I had and bought a little iPod and downloaded all of the audio books I could afford. I figured that would keep my mind stimulated while working.

Next, my thoughts turned to the physical aspect of the job. It was manual labor and it was definitely hard, but it got easier over time as my muscles got used to it. I was getting up at four thirty in the morning every day to get a more complete workout, which is something I truly enjoyed. However, I had to admit, the sheer number of hours I was active was starting to become exhausting. I was suddenly hit by an aha moment. What if the lumberyard was my gym? There were so many different types of lumber and equipment all around me that the possibilities seemed endless. I could do a deep squat after stacking a pile of lumber and a side lunge as I picked up more. I could do a back fly or a bicep curl while lifting. All of a sudden, I started to feel a renewed excitement about going to work.

My perspective was starting to change from the audio books and extra physical activity, but I still wasn't at my original level of excitement. How could I incorporate more things I loved into my daily reality to give it deeper meaning? This seemed a little tricky, especially since I was just stacking piles of wood.

I decided to create a list of everything I loved to do, in hopes that I would be able to recognize more elements of those things that were present in my job. In addition to learning and working out, I love new experiences, adventure, exploring, the outdoors, people, and growing. Working down the list, I realized a lot of these elements were part of my job already, but I had overlooked them. Instead of mentally escaping while I was at work, I could become more present by appreciating the things I liked.

For example, this job was an adventure, doing something out of the ordinary for me, and it was helping me grow as a person. In addition to that, I got to be outside every day, and the area around the lumberyard was incredibly beautiful. There were mountain peaks over the trees, and the sky was usually a stunningly clear blue. The air was crisp and clean, and the temperature was typically perfect. When I stopped to think about it, the working conditions were actually quite pleasant. I made it a point to remind myself of this several times each day.

After making these simple adjustments to my workday, I noticed an immediate difference in my outlook. The little changes worked together to make one big exponential change in my life. I didn't feel burned out anymore. I fell in love with stacking lumber, because I was able to discover how it could be rewarding to me mentally, emotionally, and physically on another level.

It's possible to make the best of tough situations and get through them. As you work toward building your ideal life, you will inevitably encounter times when you want nothing more than to press fast-forward and skip ahead to better things. Unfortunately, that isn't always possible. Instead of giving up, tossing in the towel, and walking away, take a moment for personal reflection. By shifting your perspective, you can find a deeper purpose to motivate you. When you can fall in love with your current situation, you will always have control of your life, and everything else will seem easy!

LIVE IT CHALLENGE

Is there any major area of life that you are struggling with currently or that you have struggled with in the past? Would you be a happier person if you could shift your perspective and become more positive about that area of your life?

Once you have identified an area that you want to make a shift in, answer these questions:

1. Are there elements about this aspect of your life that you used to love? Have you overlooked the parts that you find enjoyable? Try to focus on the good things.

2. What could you change to make it more interesting? Could you incorporate something new that you love?

3. How could you make it more enjoyable mentally or emotionally?

4. How could you physically go about it in a way that would help you enjoy it more?

5. What deep purpose and meaning could you add to it?

CHAPTER 6:

THE THREE OPPONENTS

f the world today had only a hundred people, here's what it would add up to:

- Eighty-three people would be able to read and write, and seventeen would not.

- Seven would have a college education; ninety-three would not.

- Twenty-two would own or share a computer; eighty-eight would not.

- Seventy-seven people would have food and shelter; twenty-three would not.

- One person would be dying of starvation, fifteen people would be undernourished, and twenty-one would be over-weight.

- Eighty-seven would have access to drinking water, and thirteen people would not.[1]

In the spring of 2004, after three months of learning how to fall in love with hard work at the lumberyard, I boarded the MV *Explorer* in Vancouver, Canada, to start my voyage around the world. During this adventure, I got to experience the aforementioned statistics firsthand—not only hearing the numbers, but seeing the reality of these disparities through my own eyes. This experience forever changed my outlook on life.

The Journey

The trip was organized to connect us with local people at each port of call so that we could see what daily life was like. We went on some fun adventures that attract tourists and locals alike, but we also spent a lot of time off the beaten path.

We started our trip in Asia, and we were excited to see how different the cultures would be from the United States. We visited Osaka, Japan, and found Japanese people to be generous and extremely hospitable. Compared to a lot of cities in the United States, everything seemed a little smaller in Osaka because of the available space. We noticed the homes were small, even for people who were well off. We learned that the Japanese cherish the time they spend with their family, but for many working people, the amount of time is limited. The Japanese workday starts early in the morning and goes late into the evening, as evidenced by the rush hour at ten o'clock in the evening. Like many Americans, Japanese people can find their jobs pulling them away from time spent with family.

Next, we visited Beijing, China, and were surprised by how many millions of people could fit into a fast-paced, energized city. There seemed to be something crammed into every square inch of Beijing. A fascinating mix of ancient traditions and new technology gave Beijing a character that the United States was too young to have. As in Japan, we learned that the family unit in China was seen as extremely important, and often three generations would live under one roof.

We made our way through Asia with a few more stops along the way, including Vietnam and Thailand. We met people who didn't have much money but were living happy lives with their family in a deeply rooted community. As different as these cities were from the United States, there were many aspects that seemed the same. I felt myself starting to see how culture makes our societies different, but at our core, human beings share more similarities than differences.

The next few stops turned my world upside down and brought those facts and figures we highlighted earlier to life.

In India, we saw hundreds and hundreds of people sleeping outside on the ground at night because they had nowhere else to go. Human beings were eating scraps of food and crumbs left on the street because there was no other food for them to eat. Many places lacked access to plumbing or outhouses, so human waste was dangerously close to—and sometimes mixed in with—the drinking water and food.

We visited rural villages in Tanzania, where people were living in mud huts with thatched roofs. During the six-month rainy season they were unable to keep the water out of their huts, so they were forced to live and sleep in wet and muddy conditions. We learned that the locals were also lacking clean drinking water and enough food to eat. Through a conversation with a volunteer nurse, I learned that hundreds of thousands of Africans were dying of malaria every year because they couldn't afford the medicine.² I couldn't believe this was happening, when the medicine costs as little as two dollars.

In a township just outside of Cape Town, South Africa, we were guided through the different parts of town and introduced to many local people. They shared life stories with us and kindly invited us into their homes. Many of their houses were quite simple, made out of four tin walls and a tin roof. Some houses had a bed, and most people had just a small handful of belongings. Once, we were invited to an apartment that was no larger than a small college dorm room. We peeked our heads into the room and noticed there were two small single beds, a miniature refrigerator, and shelves with random belongings on them, and we were told that this was a two-family room. I remember wondering what that meant. The guide later let us know that two families of five lived in that small apartment. Each family consisted of a mother, father, and three kids, all of whom slept on a single bed. I was shocked just thinking of how that was possible.

As the shock of the living conditions for so many people around the world started to hit me, my heart began to crack open and fill with disbelief. How could the rest of the world allow this to happen? People dying from dehydration, malnutrition, and a lack of basic resources. Well, "basic" was how we referred to those resources back home, but I was beginning to see how many people around the world don't have access to the resources we take for granted.

After more than three months, the journey finally came to an end. Even though I was only traveling for one semester, it felt like I had started the voyage a whole lifetime ago. I didn't realize it at the time, but I had transformed into a different person during the trip.

When I returned home and settled in, I experienced a massive culture shock. I tried to get back into doing the routine things I used to enjoy, but it wasn't the same. Conversations with my friends began to seem boring and devoid of meaning. The problems they were challenged with in their lives now seemed trivial and silly compared to what my classmates and I had seen during our travels. Going back to school at the University of San Diego so I could graduate and get a normal job felt pointless. All I could think about was how there were people in the world who were suffering and dying on a daily basis due to lack of simple resources. After countless nights of dreaming about people who were less fortunate and hours contemplating the reality of poverty in the world, I finally decided I couldn't sit back any longer and watch it happen.

At this point in my life, donating money seemed like a nice gesture, but I didn't have much to spare. Starting a not-for-profit organization seemed like too big of a task and would take way too long. The only option that made sense to me was to pick an organization to partner with and head over to start finding a way to make a difference.

I found an organization called Students Partnership Worldwide (now called Restless Development). It organizes volunteer trips to developing countries to help out in a variety of ways. I was intrigued by the program in Uganda where volunteers teach organic farming skills to rural farmers. I didn't know anything about farming, but the program promised to teach the volunteers everything they needed to know. I decided to sign up.

When I told my friends and family about signing up to volunteer, I expected they would be excited for me. I was making a huge life choice to step outside of my comfort zone, learn a lot of new skills, have experiences that would benefit me personally and professionally, and most importantly, give back to people in need. What's not to be excited about, right?

Unfortunately, a lot of the reactions were not what I had anticipated. Friends and family members brought up all kinds of reasons why it might not be a good idea to go on the volunteer trip. I had already considered some of their points, but they also brought up new worries I hadn't even thought of. I tried to let their words roll off my back, but it was hard. Some of the comments from the people closest to me really got to me and made me question my own decision.

Many people go through this same thing when they make major life decisions. As you set forth on your path of turning your real life into your ideal life, you will make decisions that surprise and even shock your friends and family. Their perspectives can turn into opponents that keep you from chasing your dreams. It is important to be aware of these opponents in advance so that you can stay on track more easily and feel confident about your course of action. Rather than being knocked off track when you are met with skepticism and doubt, you will realize that these reactions are normal, and they don't need to affect the decisions you have already made for yourself.

There are three different types of opponents you are likely to encounter. Here we will examine each one, explain why the opponents exist in the first place, and provide tips to overcome them.

Outside Opponents

Outside Opponents are acquaintances, coworkers, distant relatives, mentors, people in your community, and even some of your friends. You might have coffee or lunch with these people every now and then, but you aren't close enough for them to truly understand the depths of who you are. You know a fair amount of what is going on in their lives at the surface, but you don't know what makes them tick.

When I was planning my trip to Uganda, I realized that a lot of my friends and classmates were Outside Opponents. I remember a conversation I had with a bunch of them when we were hanging out one day. I asked them how they were doing and what was new, and they went around the circle and talked about some drama on TV, what celebrities were doing, a fun trip they had scheduled, and some cool party on their to-do list. This was back in college, so it was a normal conversation.

When they turned to me and it was my turn to share what I was up to, I told them how excited I was about recently signing up for a six-month volunteer program in Uganda. I shared how I would be living in a rural village without electricity or running water, but it would be worth it because I would be giving back and making a difference. I talked about how I would be teaching organic farming and helping people till the soil and grow natural live foods so their village could become healthy and start thriving.

At first, my friends soaked up a little of what I was saying, but after a few minutes of trying to digest my story, they didn't agree with it. They started poking holes in my plans and asking questions like the following:

"It seems kind of ridiculous to travel all the way out there. Aren't there other people already helping them?"

"Don't you want to stay focused and graduate from school? If you move there and you don't like it, what happens? What if you decide you don't want to come back? Isn't it more important to stay here, finish your college education, and get your degree?"

"Why don't you wait until you get a job, grow up, and have a family, and then when you're ready to retire, go help those people?"

My friends had idea after idea about why I was making a bad decision, and they piled those opinions on top of me in an avalanche of negativity. Stepping outside of my comfort zone had clearly pulled them outside of their comfort zones as well. I expected to feel encouraged by sharing my plans with them, but instead I felt frustrated and misunderstood.

Have you ever felt this way when you told people about a new plan in your life? Maybe you wanted to start a new diet or fitness regimen, go back to school, change careers, or have a baby. Whatever your plan, you had already made up your mind on what you were going to do, and you were excited about not only moving forward, but sharing the good news with others. Instead of having people offer encouragement, they were skeptical, which was disappointing to you.

The reason for this reaction isn't because your friends want to bring you down; they just don't want to believe there are options in the world beyond the ones they have already chosen for themselves. People often develop a crystal-clear perspective on how they believe life should be lived: where you should start, what you should do next, and what the journey should look like. This vision works for them, in their world, because it's modeled after what they see around them. Family and close friends create norms for daily life and long-term goals, which make it hard for people to envision life any other way. When you share your ideas with people who already have their minds made up on how to live life, they consider whether your vision matches theirs. When it doesn't match, they'll resist understanding your perspective, because they don't want to believe there is another way to live. They believe their way is right, and accepting another option feels akin to admitting they could have made other (and possibly better) choices.

Although Outside Opponents can be difficult to deal with, they are typically the easiest of the three opponents to overcome.

Intimate Opponents

Intimate Opponents are the people closest to you in life: your significant other, husband, wife, kids, mom, dad, and best friends. These are the people who know who you are at the core, and they understand your motivation. Unlike Outside Opponents, Intimate Opponents hold your well-being as the top priority. In fact, they are often more averse to you taking risks that could jeopardize your well-being than you are!

When I decided to go to Uganda, I learned this the hard way. I thought my family and friends might have some reservations about my plan, but I figured they would be initially supportive. I expected my mom and grandma to respond with something like "Oh my gosh! That's so amazing. Good for you. We're so proud of you. You're going to make such a big difference. Is there any way we can help?"

Caring about their opinions and wanting so badly to get their approval made it that much harder to hear their concerns. Each person I told went down the list of objections, rattling off every reason why he or she thought I was making a bad decision. It sounded something like this: "What if you get kidnapped? What if you get sick? Do they have good hospitals? Is it dangerous? What if you get beaten up? What if they steal your stuff? You could die there!"

Although my family and close friends had a myriad of reasons why they thought I shouldn't go, I realized how different their thought process was than that of my Outside Opponents. It wasn't about whether my model of the world matched theirs. It was all about the fear of loss, the fear of losing me. They didn't want to worry about something bad happening to me—someone who was so important to them, someone they loved so much. They were scared of me living on the other side of the world, too far for them to help me if I were in trouble.

Like Outside Opponents, Intimate Opponents consider their own worldview when they assess another person's plans. However, instead of trying to uphold the status quo for social norms, they focus on the beliefs they hold about safety, health, and overall well-being. These standards for personal welfare guide people through life, and they are hard to challenge.

Think about it: When people you love make choices that go against what you consider to be healthy or safe, don't you have the urge to step in and stop them? You feel emotionally invested in their well-being, and you want to make sure they are OK. Even when you hear more about why they think they are making good choices, it is unlikely you will change your mind about what you think is healthy or safe.

Considering this, it's easy to see how Intimate Opponents can put up a good fight when it comes to getting their point across. They have the emotional fuel to get their way, and on top of that, they know you well enough to target your soft spots. They know exactly what to say to make you doubt yourself and your choices. Although Intimate Opponents can sometimes have outlandish fears, they have your safety at heart, which makes it hard to discredit their objections. That's why Intimate Opponents are typically the cause of setting up your third and final opponent.

The Internal Opponent

The final opponent you might encounter on your journey is *you*. It's that little voice in your head that says, "Do you really know what you are doing? Do you truly understand what you've gotten yourself into? Are you sure this is going to work out the way you imagine?"

The Internal Opponent likes to strike when we least expect it, often after we've overcome Outside and Intimate Opponents. It can be hard to shake off other people's doubts, and sometimes we internalize them even when we're trying our hardest to stay strong. After hearing so many people poke holes in our plans, it's easy to lose certainty and faith in our vision. It can begin to feel like we're moving backward into a tunnel of doubt.

I experienced this when I decided to go to Uganda. Even though I stood up to my Outside and Intimate Opponents in person, a little voice in my head told me later that maybe they were right.

When you start to head down the path of questioning goals that you once held with total certainty, it puts you in a bad place.

The best way to safeguard yourself from this opponent is to pre-pare for it.

Creating positive habits will help you build certainty and determination that is strong enough to withstand doubt. Structuring these habits and sticking to them will turn your habits into rituals, which become second nature to follow.

"All truth passes through three stages. First, it is ridiculed. Second, it is violently opposed. Third, it is accepted as being self-evident."
—*attributed to Arthur Schopenhauer*[3]

In the meantime, you have to find your truth. Your truth is your guiding light through all of the resistance. Here are the elements that make up your personal T.R.U.T.H.:

T—You must have a clear and defined *trajectory*. Your Ideal Day vision will work great for this!

R—You have to be willing to *rebuke* the naysayers, *renounce* their doubts, and be *relentless* in your approach.

U—You'll have to be *unconventional* with your strategies, *unified* in your internal thoughts and beliefs, and *unassailable*.

T—You'll need a massive amount of *tenacity* to ensure you will be able to take the punches and continue to make progress no matter what life tosses your way.

H—You will need to create a place you can go each day to refuel. Use your daily *habits* to create your mental, emotional, and physical safe *haven*. This will help you feel like your world is in total *harmony*. *morning anchors*

LIVE IT CHALLENGE

1. What can you do each day to apply the T.R.U.T.H. formula in your life and business?

2. What are the daily habits and rituals you can use to keep yourself focused and on track?

CHAPTER 7:

YOU ARE NOT GUARANTEED A TOMORROW

"It's not death that man should fear, but he should fear never beginning to live."
—*Marcus Aurelius, Roman emperor*[1]

We all know on some level that we are not guaranteed a tomorrow. Eventually our life here on earth will come to an end, and our existence as we know it will never be the same. When that happens, all of the possessions we have accumulated will no longer belong to us. All of the money, fame, and recognition will become a fading memory. The one thing that will be remembered is the difference we made in the lives of the people around us.

The thought of death is not meant to be unpleasant or burdensome—it is a simple reminder of the truth. Although we know dying is one of the few guarantees in life, it makes most people uncomfortable to think about it. But remembering that our time is limited can actually play a major role in deciding how we spend that time. Many people will go through a major health scare at some point in their lives, where they question whether life will suddenly be cut short. The same holds true for people who survive bad accidents or dangerous situations. Often people describe those traumatic events as "a wake-up call." They remember that life is a gift that shouldn't be taken for granted, and that realization many times causes them to change their lives for the better. I know this firsthand, and I am living my life differently because of it.

I would never wish a health scare or near-death experience on anyone, but I have to say honestly that I was shocked by the amount of clarity I gained through my experience. The clarity that it brought to my life helped me make the most out of every moment and opportunity. Contemplating your mortality can transform your outlook in positive ways—a wake-up call for some and a reminder for others.

My Turning Point

In deciding whether to volunteer in Uganda I used my T.R.U.T.H. to guide me in my vision. I defied my opponents and decided to go. My volunteer group was focused on spreading knowledge about organic farming techniques, and we were stationed in the rural countryside in a pineapple farming village called Kangulumira. We were trained in rural organic farming techniques, with the purpose of sharing this knowledge with numerous villages in the area so they could improve their crops, land, and local village economy.

We were told that the reason we were needed in the farming villages was that a few years prior, companies from the United States and the United Kingdom had come to Uganda and sold the farmers a harmful pesticide to use on crops. The pesticide was known to be dangerous, and it had been illegal in both the United States and the United Kingdom for eleven years because it kills crops, poisons the soil, and even poisons the food grown in the soil. However, the companies didn't tell that to the people of Uganda when they sold them barrels and barrels of this product. Sure enough, it killed crops, poisoned the soil, and destroyed the local economy of these villages.

Our main goal in being there was to help farmers and communities start producing food again in safe ways. We went from village to village and gave lectures and workshops on the fundamental elements needed to replenish the land. We were determined to make a difference, and we did our best to help the local villagers to improve their situation.

It was inspiring how eager people were for knowledge and how fast they absorbed the concepts and were able to apply them to their lives and businesses. They were incredibly grateful for the knowledge and were excited to be able to take it back to their own villages and share it with all the others to help get their local economy back on track.

Along with our day-to-day work in the villages, we also did our best to squeeze in some leisure activities while we were there, including a memorable excursion in white-water rafting down the Nile River. This rafting trip set the wheels in motion for the turning point in my life. The night before our trip, we had to stay close to where the rafting organization was going to pick us up in the morning. We all met up at the hostel, and as we got ready for bed, I realized that I was the only one who had forgotten my mosquito net for that night.

I'll never forget going to the bathroom at two in the morning and seeing one side of my face twice the normal size. I had been bitten in the face by a mosquito, and judging by the swelling, I could only assume that it was carrying a common illness in Uganda, such as malaria, dengue fever, typhoid fever, or yellow fever.

I woke up the next morning not feeling too great, but the swelling had gone down a little, which made me feel a bit hopeful. I still went rafting and had fun, even though I didn't feel well. The next few days I didn't feel so hot either, but I mentally wrote it off as just being sore from the rafting.

When feeling tired, sore, and beaten up continued past a week and a half, I decided to go to the local clinic, where the doctor diagnosed me with malaria. I was given the option of malaria medication that came in the form of a shot or pills.

You might be wondering why I didn't already have a malaria vaccination. I grew up in Southern California in a family that passionately believed our bodies would heal themselves through natural remedies. We avoided taking pills, shots, or any other form of standard medicine, so I had never gotten the vaccines most Americans get, including the vaccines that are recommended when going abroad. I wasn't sure if the doctor's diagnosis was correct, but even if it was, I thought I could heal myself without medicine. I asked the doctor to prescribe me the malaria pills so he wouldn't hassle me, but I decided not to take them.

Things didn't go as well as I had planned. Each day I felt a little sorer and a little more tired. After a couple of weeks I began to feel like my mind was cloudy, and about a month later I found myself lying on the ground with a fever like I'd never had in my life. Thank God a few of the little children in the village noticed me lying on the ground and went to get a bucket of water and a rag to help cool me down. I was dizzy and nauseated, and eventually I hit a point where I had trouble breathing. I started to believe the doctor from the clinic had diagnosed me correctly. Because I had refused the medicine and had let it get worse, I honestly wasn't sure what options I had left, but I still did not take the malaria medicine.

One of the volunteer members in my group saw what I was going through, decided enough was enough, and called an ambulance. It seemed like an eternity, but an ambulance was sent out for me and drove me to the hospital in the closest major city, Jinja. That doctor decided to send me to another clinic in Entebbe that specialized in malaria and was run by a European doctor.

He took a blood sample, and a few minutes later he returned to let me know that the village doctor was correct, and I did in fact have malaria in my blood. He told me that the best way to get rid of it would be to take the malaria shot. I told him that I would happily decline and asked if there was a natural approach to get rid of it. He seemed a bit frustrated and did his best to understand why I was so passionate about not taking the shot.

After about twenty minutes of going back and forth on our beliefs about medicine, he decided to just lay the options out visually for me to see. He took a live sample of my blood and put it up on the screen in front of me. On the screen, he highlighted that according to the test, there were roughly fifty-five thousand parasites per one red blood cell. He explained to me what malaria was and how it works. He said that the malaria parasites lay eggs inside red blood cells, which hatch every eight to ten hours. This means the parasites double quickly and repeatedly. He explained that according to the current count per red blood cell and the rate at which they were doubling, I would have only "about five days to go."

I blurted out, "Five days to go where?"

He smiled sympathetically and said, "Five days until there will be so many malaria parasites in your blood and so many red blood cells depleted that your body will no longer be able to sustain itself."

I tried to process that information, but I was shaken up and confused. I thought my body could heal itself without Western medicine, no matter what. Up until that point, it always had. In that moment, however, my certainty was cracked. I decided to call home and ask for some advice.

I called Dad first. I told him the situation and he said, "You'll be fine. Do whatever you believe with 100 percent certainty, and that is what will heal you. If you believe your mind will heal you, your mind will heal you. If you believe the medicine will heal you, take it, and the medicine will heal you. But whichever you believe, do it now and do it with certainty!"

Well, that wasn't much help, because he didn't really tell me what to do. So I decided to call Mom, and I got a much different response. She said, "I didn't raise you for eighteen years so you can go die in some godforsaken country on the other side of the world! Take that medicine! I am on my way!" and she hung up the phone. I remember laughing and thinking she wasn't going to be happy when she got here. After thinking long and hard, I decided to take the medicine, just in case.

The next week proved to be the most painful and scary week of my life. The medicine caused the malaria parasites to hatch all at once, instead of in waves like they had been hatching for the past month. The doctor told me that this would increase the level of active parasites, thus increasing the pain. He said it would feel like a sledgehammer to the gut, and boy was he right.

I was told the medicine should save my life, but I wasn't so sure, especially because I felt so close to death. Food or water wouldn't stay down, because I was throwing up and having diarrhea. I became dehydrated and had vertigo. I had to crawl to the bathroom because I couldn't walk. My body was going through fits of hot and cold, where one moment I was roasting hot and the next minute I was freezing cold. It left me going back and forth between taking off my clothes, putting on my clothes, taking off my clothes, putting on my clothes, and then throwing up.

Despite my level of extreme physical pain and discomfort, the inability to escape my own thoughts was even worse. There was a very real chance that I wasn't going to make it. It wasn't the thought of death that scared me most—it was the fear of not ever having really lived. I lay there for hours and hours thinking about everything I wanted to accomplish, experience, and achieve in my life. Up until that point, I thought I had lived a full life, but getting sick made me realize how much I had left that I wanted to do. I thought about the big stuff, like finding the love of my life, getting married, having kids, and seeing my family again. I also thought about the little stuff, like finishing college, delivering on promises I had made, starting a business, and buying a house. Suddenly, what I wanted in life seemed clearer than it ever had before. It seemed ironic that my mind and emotions waited until now to make their greatest desires abundantly clear. As I lay there, I knew if I survived malaria, I would never live my life the same.

I hate to spoil the surprise, but thanks to the medicine, I survived this experience. As a result of coming face-to-face with death, I saw life in a new way. This newfound perspective allowed me to better assess whether my actions were a reflection of my true priorities and values. Since we aren't guaranteed a tomorrow, was I living my life so that if I died suddenly, I would feel good about how I had spent my time and proud of what I had accomplished? Did I really live the life of my dreams? Did I take time to go out and experience everything in my ideal day? At that point, the answer for me was no. I came to the realization that if I would have regrets if I died tomorrow, I was doing something wrong.

After going through that experience and seeing how my viewpoint changed, I wanted to help others experience this change in perspective. I created a variety of tools and examples to use with my one-on-one coaching clients, and I saw how helpful they were in providing a new outlook.

Gratitude

The thing that was most upsetting to me when I was faced with death was that I finally realized how fortunate I was to be living such a great life filled with people I loved, but I had taken it all for granted. Up until that point, I thought I appreciated what I had. If someone asked me if I was lucky, I would have said yes and meant it. But I didn't really spend time every day *feeling* lucky. I didn't focus my attention or energy on gratitude. Gratitude was floating around in my subconscious and it would come out in certain situations, but it was often a fleeting emotion. I realized that if I had been able to focus more on being grateful for things in the moment, I would have been a happier person.

What a revelation! By making a small change to my outlook, I could transform the way I experienced life. I want to be clear that this change wasn't forced. My near-death experience simply caused me to see how abundant my life really was. I had people who loved me, enough food to eat, and the freedom to make my own choices. I had absolutely everything I needed and more. Even during times when I felt frustrated, it was now easy to see how my blessings outnumbered and outweighed my challenges.

The biggest change was how I suddenly made a shift in my behavior. Taking things for granted is a key reason people procrastinate instead of focusing on improvement. They think they can put things off and the opportunity will always be there. Obviously, this isn't true. Now that I had a clear perspective on what was most important to me, my actions started better aligning with my priorities.

I remembered learning in school that gratitude is a powerful tool people can use to improve their mental, emotional, and physical health, but now I understood how that was truly possible. Becoming aware of how much I appreciated the world around me made me feel like a whole new person—a better person. I had gone through a horrible experience where I almost died, but somehow I was better because of it.

My hope is that you never have to face a moment like I did to experience immense gratitude for life. On the journey of turning your current life into your ideal life, it's important to be grateful for what you have in the here and now, instead of always focusing on what you want to have in the future. Having goals is a key to success, but if you aren't working at becoming the best you at this moment in time, it will be much harder for you to reach your goals. When you are able to focus on the positives in life and feel grateful, you open the door to vast improvements.

Numerous studies have been conducted on the effects of gratitude, and the results prove that people who show a higher level of gratitude are happier; have more energy, determination, and enthusiasm; and experience less stress, anxiety, and depression than those who show lower levels of gratitude. People who are grateful also tend to get more sleep and exercise more often than others.[2]

While it's proven that being grateful is good for your health, sometimes it's hard to flip a switch and change your perspective, especially in the absence of a health or safety crisis that changes who you are at the core. Luckily, there are steps you can take to proactively improve your gratitude.

LIVE IT CHALLENGE

A study showed that people who kept a daily journal of what they were grateful for were able to reshape their outlook and actually become more grateful. However, it is important to note that being grateful isn't an exercise in comparing circumstances. Participants in the research study who kept a journal on why they were better off than others, instead of why they were grateful, did not experience an increase in gratitude or the benefits associated with higher levels of gratitude. This shows the importance of taking the next step and feeling thankful, instead of simply recognizing that things could be worse.

Start a gratitude journal and write down at least one thing you are grateful for each day. Hopefully over time you will be able to take that one thing each day you are grateful for and turn it into a never-ending list. Increasing gratitude takes practice just like any other skill. When you are able to become more aware of how blessed you truly are, it will be easier for you to keep working at turning your current life into your ideal life.

Values

It may sound like a cliché, but when I was faced with death, my whole life flashed before me. It made me contemplate what was really important in my life and what I valued. Identifying your personal values is necessary for living your life to the fullest, so it's good to think about them before you're faced with your own mortality! Your values will provide a frame of reference for looking at the world and help guide your behavior down the right path.

According to sociologist Morris Massey, there are three periods when people develop their values.[3] These values tell us what is important, beneficial, helpful, and admirable. They also become our framework for deciding what is wrong, useless, embarrassing, or silly. It helps for us to understand these times in our lives and how our values back then played a part in shaping our opinions in adulthood.

Imprint period—From birth to seven years—young children are like sponges, absorbing everything around them and accepting much of it as true. Parents are especially influential.

Modeling period—From eight to thirteen years—older children are still quite impressionable, but the period of blind acceptance switches to copying people. Teachers and parents play a role in shaping viewpoints.

Socialization period—From thirteen to twenty-one years—teenagers and young adults are largely influenced by their peers, and they seek out people and groups who are like them.

Massey believes that most people's value systems are set in place by the age of twenty-one and will be guided by significant emotional events from that point on.

Thinking back on how you have changed since childhood, you can probably see how most of your core values were created at a young age. You have likely changed your mind over the years about what is "cool" or "uncool," but the most important things in life were shaped mostly by the people around you and your own life experiences.

As a next step and exercise, it is important to identify your values. Take out your notepad and make a list of what you value most in life. If you aren't sure where to start, think back to Chapter 2, where we covered the majors. Some of the things that are most important to you might be included in that chapter. Another place to look would be your Ideal Day vision from Chapter 1. What was most important to you about that day? The people, places, emotions, or activities? What elements, if excluded from that vision, would make it so it wasn't your ideal day? That should help give you a hint toward what you value most.

- Identify the top ten aspects of your life that you value most.

- Next, put the list in order of importance.

Remember that people have unique values, and we aren't searching for one "right" answer here. The most important part of this exercise is that you answer thoughtfully and honestly.

After you've finished making your list, you can set it aside for now. We will pick it back up in the next chapter. Make sure you complete this exercise before moving on.

Time Management—Action versus Reaction

Since our time in this world is limited, how we manage our time is of the utmost importance. Time management is an essential skill for happiness and success in all aspects of life. Some people are naturally good at it, while it takes a little more work for others. No matter where you are on the spectrum, know that your ability to manage your time will shape your life experience. You can either accomplish what is most important to you or get pulled in a hundred different directions and feel like you never have anything to show for it.

Action versus reaction is a key differentiator in using time wisely. Do you go out every single day and choose what you will do and where you will go, and do your best to stay on track and make it happen? Or do you wake up and allow the demands of life to push and pull you all around town?

According to author Stephen Covey, there are four different "quadrants" people can live in as far as their day-to-day lives and time management are concerned. People focus on different types of tasks in each quadrant:

Quadrant 1—Important and urgent

Quadrant 2—Important but not urgent

Quadrant 3—Urgent but not important

Quadrant 4—Not urgent and not important[4]

The key to improving your time management skills is to train yourself to live predominantly in Quadrant 2, what Covey refers to as the "quadrant of leadership," which includes tasks that are important but not yet urgent in your life and business. This is challenging, however, because the world wants you to work on its clock, which is often considered Quadrant 3, "urgent but not important." People want your attention right now—your co-workers, family, friends, acquaintances, and salespeople, and the list goes on and on. A lot of the items they are bringing to your attention aren't important to you, but nonetheless, these people want an immediate response from you. This quadrant of distraction will leave you constantly putting out fires and stuck in a reactive mode. If you get caught up in these minor things, you will never get to the important things.

To avoid getting derailed by frequent interruptions, make sure you have a plan for effectively managing your time. Do you have a time management system, such as a FranklinCovey planner or a Rapid Planning Method planner, which you use to manage and organize the hours of your day? Do you block off time on your calendar each day to get your most important tasks completed? Or set reminder alerts for yourself? These methods will all help you live a life of action and intention, instead of reaction and distraction.

The Live It List

You're probably familiar with the term *bucket list*—a list of things people want to see, do, and accomplish before they die, a.k.a. "kick the bucket." Unfortunately, bucket lists don't work, because most people avoid thinking about dying, and they choose to exist in a mind-set in which they still have plenty of time left. When I had malaria and was close to dying, I remember thinking about how my bucket list was virtually untouched. I didn't have any sense of urgency to accomplish my goals on that list, because I thought I had my whole life ahead of me.

Procrastinating on bucket lists is actually quite similar to how people put off New Year's resolutions, which are notoriously ineffective. Even though there's a set end date for a New Year's resolution, it seems so far away that there's no harm in putting it off until tomorrow, or next week, or next month. Pretty soon, it's hard to remember what the resolution was, let alone have enough time left at the end to accomplish it.

Using the concept of the bucket list, I came up with the Live It List, which is like a bucket list except it focuses on achieving various goals within shorter timeframes. Unlike regular bucket lists, the Live It List ensures you keep your goals in mind, and it makes you accountable for reaching them within a predetermined time-frame. Instead of being overwhelmed by how many things you want to accomplish over the course of your life, you can view that list in bite-sized chunks.

Think of this technique like running a marathon, where the finish line symbolizes your long-term vision and big goals. The mile markers symbolize shorter periods of time within your life, such as five to ten years. Marathon runners use mile markers to gauge their progress, and most have a goal of exactly how long it should take them to reach each mile marker. Let's say you have a goal of running a marathon in three hours and thirty minutes. That would mean in order to be on track with your goal, you would have to maintain a pace of roughly eight minutes per mile. When runners reach mile one, they will be in one of the following situations:

1. They arrive behind schedule and they need to speed up.

2. They arrive on schedule and they can continue to keep pace.

3. They arrive ahead of schedule and they can either continue to beat their goal time or they can ease up a bit for the next mile.

When you can break up your goals into a series of mini goals, like a marathon runner, those goals suddenly become much more manageable. It is also easier to tell if you are going at the right pace.

For example, if going to Paris is on your bucket list, that can seem like a pretty big item to tackle. Where do you even start? However, if you break that goal down into the steps needed in order to accomplish it, then it suddenly seems a lot easier. Instead of putting it off, it's easier to stay organized and on track by marking off each task individually. Your new Live It List might look something like this:

- Start saving seventy-five dollars per month and keep this money separate from other savings.

- Research the best time of the year to visit Paris, and narrow down a time frame for traveling.

- Decide whom to invite on the trip.

- Apply for a passport.

- Research hotels.

- Book flights and hotel.

- Learn important words and phrases in French.

- Bon voyage!

Now you have a much clearer sense of direction on what you need to do in order to make your dream trip to Paris a reality. Next, you would assign each item a deadline for completion. The trick is not thinking about these as flexible deadlines you can put off; instead, think of them the same way as you would with a marathon. If you start to fall behind your pace time at the mile markers, it becomes more and more difficult to catch up later. There will be no surprises down the road that you're way behind—you'll know you're losing steam as it's happening, so you can work harder to catch up.

LIVE IT CHALLENGE

In order to start using your Live It List, you need to have a regular bucket list first. You probably already have a few things in mind, even if you've never written them down. Take some time now to make a list of what you want to accomplish in your life. It might be helpful to think back to the majors and work your way through those categories.

Next, you need to prioritize the urgency of these goals so you know what to work on first. Since you aren't guaranteed a tomorrow, what would you be most disappointed to miss on your list? Use that as your number-one goal. Now work your way through all the goals and put them in order. Depending on how many goals are on your list and how in-depth your work will be in meeting these goals, you can set a pace for yourself. You should always be working on one of your goals!

Five Regrets of the Dying

Although learning from experience is sometimes the best route, when it comes to living a full life, we can learn from others. I came across an interesting study that was conducted by Bronnie Ware, a palliative nurse who cared for patients who were near the end of their lives.[5] She asked her patients whether they had any regrets or whether they would do anything differently if they could go back in time. In asking people this question, she hoped to gain wisdom on how to live a more fulfilled life. When her patients responded, she noticed common themes coming up again and again.

As you work to create your ideal life, keep the following regrets in mind. Since they are so commonly shared by people who are nearing the end of their lives, it is easy to see how people have the propensity to live in a way that would cause these regrets.

1. I wish I'd had the courage to live a life true to myself, not the life others expected of me.

This was the most common regret. People thought back on all of their dreams that were left unfulfilled because of choices they made.

Don't wait until it's too late to go for what you really want in life. Hopefully you have taken time to design your Ideal Day vision and have been working each day toward turning that vision into reality.

2. I wish I hadn't worked so hard.

Every male patient Ware interviewed shared this regret. (Since many patients were elderly and a large percentage of women didn't work outside the home, Ware cites this reason for the difference in responses by gender.)

Of course it is important to have the financial means to support yourself and your family, but take note that "I wish I had made more money" is not a top regret. By simplifying your lifestyle and making conscious choices along the way, it is possible to not need the income that you think you do.

Another amazing opportunity that has come about in the last few years is the ability to build an online business and give yourself the freedom to work from anywhere in the world via a computer. Working from home is an opportunity that many companies are offering to their employees as well. This can allow you to spend more time with the ones you love versus spending it on a long commute to and from an office.

3. I wish I'd had the courage to express my feelings.

Many patients said they suppressed their feelings because they wanted to uphold positive relationships with others. However, by keeping their opinions bottled up, they felt they had missed out on taking a chance at living a more authentic life. When you say what's on your mind, you run the risk of people responding unfavorably, but you open the door to improving relationships in the long run.

4. I wish I had stayed in touch with my friends.

People thought back on all of the friendships they had over the course of their lives, and they regretted not taking the initiative to keep relationships going. Make sure you're taking the time to nurture the relationships you have with friends, even when life gets busy.

5. I wish that I had let myself be happier.

Ware said that most of her patients didn't realize until the end of their lives that happiness is a choice. They got caught up in making it through their day-to-day existence, even if it wasn't making them happy.

Happiness is hard to measure, so it's easy to forget how much it matters. Remember that it is your choice to be happy in life. One way to increase your happiness is to spend time focused on activities that are fulfilling versus those that are pleasurable. Pleasurable activities are those things you enjoy and feel good doing in the moment, but that do not add up to long-term fulfillment. Fulfilling activities are those that feel good in the moment and continue to reap positive emotional rewards in the long-term future.

Take a few moments now and think about each of these regrets. Knowing that you aren't guaranteed a tomorrow, would you share in any of these regrets if your life was cut short? If so, you need to make a change today! Your goal is to live each day in a way that makes you feel like you have made the best possible use of your time.

CHAPTER 8:

BACK IN THE MINORS

Returning home from Uganda to normal life was quite an adjustment. I felt a newfound appreciation to be returning to a part of the world where daily life is less of a struggle. I no longer had to walk a quarter mile every day to get my drinking water from the nearby well, then spend two hours boiling it so it was safe to drink and letting it cool down so it was drinkable in the summer heat. In the United States, all I had to do was turn on the faucet or stick my glass under the spout connected to the refrigerator. Growing up with running water, it's easy to take it for granted. After living without it for several months, I suddenly found myself in awe of "basic" technology. I remember looking at toilets in a whole new light: what a genius idea! Electricity is highly impressive when you stop to think about it. All you have to do is flip a switch at night and boom, you can see. In the beginning, returning to modern technology and conveniences felt great. It only added to my positive outlook.

Beyond being impressed with modern technology, I was alive and I had a new lease on life. I felt like my passion for living was on fire! I made it a point to try to do just about everything I could dream of, since I felt that I was given a second chance. I thought about the majors in my life, and I started making progress on all of them. My health needed to be more of a priority, so I spent time getting into the best shape of my life. I even decided to run a marathon. I wanted to do more fun activities with my family, so I took my mom skydiving for Mother's Day. I also decided to make giving back a bigger part of my daily life. I volunteered at a local soup kitchen and did my best to share my experiences and raise awareness for the villages in Uganda. Since I knew life didn't guarantee me a tomorrow, I wanted to make as much progress as I could as quickly as I could.

While I was accomplishing many of my goals and felt good about my progress, I found myself unable to stop thinking about what life was like in Uganda and other developing nations. It had profoundly changed my perspective on life to have no running water or electricity and to use a hole in the ground for a toilet, in a place where we saw people dying every day from lack of nutrition, clean water, and medicine. I had a new appreciation for my standard of living, but my heart went out to people who were less fortunate. We consider these resources simple, but a lot of people in the world today will never enjoy these things we take for granted. In fact, 10 percent of the world's population (780 million people) still relies on drinking water sources that haven't been improved with technology.[1]

Getting to experience life in a way that is so foreign to Americans but so common in other parts of the world opened my eyes and my heart. Things that used to be important no longer mattered. After experiencing how so many other people live, making a lot of money no longer seemed important. It's hard to focus on building a life for yourself that revolves around making more money to buy more things, when you've lived so close to people who were struggling to simply survive. What was now important didn't seem to align with what I valued before experiencing how the majority of the world lives. My personal values had changed.

Now, my only focus was on how to change the world. I believed that the way I could do it was to help people rapidly achieve their own personal goals so that they could finally forget about themselves and start focusing on ways to serve the world around them. It made no difference to me if they were going to focus on helping their family, their community, or people in developing nations around the world; I wanted to give people the opportunity to give!

Years after having this realization, I am thrilled to say I am now living my passion through the Rapid Results Retreat program I developed. These trips give people the opportunity to assess and realign their values and transform their lives to become a reflection of their mission and purpose. Since the retreats are also multiple-country tours, they allow participants to see firsthand how people in developing nations live every day. A desire to give back ignites in people's hearts when they see developing nations with their own eyes. A newfound passion for giving back isn't mandatory, but it seems to happen naturally during the trip.

I am immensely proud of the program, but less proud of how long it took me to develop it. I recognized my passion while I was in college, but it took me several years to pursue it seriously. Instead of going after what I truly wanted, I got sidetracked for years. I knew I wasn't guaranteed a tomorrow, so I started pursuing all of my dreams aggressively. I made progress, but I got stuck along the way.

Soon after I discovered my life's purpose, I heard about the World Race, a program developed by a Christian organization. It was a twelve-month, twelve-country journey around the world with a focus on volunteering and mission work. To add another element of fun for participants, teams raced each other to and from each country for prizes and bragging rights. The moment I heard about it, I knew it was meant for me. This was the journey I was meant to be on. I signed up online, made it through the interview process, and got accepted. I was ready to go!

When I told my family, they had mixed reactions. I suppose it was understandable, since I had almost died on my last international volunteer trip. The one person whom I counted on for love and support—my dad—had a different tone this time around. I told him this trip was what I had always wanted to do, and I asked for his blessing. He said, "You know, son, you've had enough adventures. It's time to finish school and get a job. It's time to grow up."

I remember hearing those words and thinking, "What does that even mean?" To be an adult in modern society, would I have to become someone who gets up early in the morning and reports to the office or wherever I'm supposed to be and spend my whole life hustling away in a life completely devoid of adventure? Earning a paycheck and then spending it on the things society tells me are important? Constantly going from month to month just trying to get by and pay bills? That version of becoming an adult didn't seem to add up in my head or my future. I knew that type of life, and unhappiness wasn't what my dad meant for me to chase, but that's what it felt like.

I respect my dad a lot and always have. He has accomplished so much in his life that I value his opinion more than just about anyone's. Even though my gut told me to go on the volunteer trip despite what any of my opponents told me, this time I took his advice and decided not to go. I called the organization and said,

"I'm so sorry, but I'm not going to be able to make this trip. I have to focus on my life." I went back and did what I was expected to do. I spent the next few years finishing my degree. When I graduated, I got a job in outside sales.

I spent the next two years going around the country leading Peak Performance workshops and presentations for my dad's company, with a goal of enrolling people into upcoming seminars. In the beginning it was fun. It was an exciting job and I had a fun time meeting new people and learning the ropes at my first full-time job. It was a nonstop, 24-7 hustle. I was so busy that I actually stopped thinking about people in developing nations every day, and for a little while, I forgot about my newfound passion.

I'll never forget the day it finally dawned on me. I had fallen back into the minors of life. Instead of focusing on the majors and how I was growing as a human being in my emotions, relationships, business, and spiritual life, I had gotten caught up in the daily routine of just getting the job done. I went to the next sales presentation to get the next sale, just trying to get my numbers up so my boss would be happy with me and my family would be proud of me. The worst part was that I realized I wasn't doing anything to work toward my Ideal Day vision I had created. It was also becoming clear that even though I had discovered what I referred to as my purpose in life, I was doing nothing to live in alignment with it.

When we find ourselves in a moment like this, it isn't a fun realization. It is a place most people try to avoid with all their might. Many people tell themselves daily that they are doing good things in the world. They are working on important projects and doing their best to be a good person. They bury themselves in busy work as an attempt to avoid having to define something that would bring deep meaning and purpose into their lives.

Living Someone Else's Dream

Falling back into the minors is tricky because it happens to people so often, and it can be pretty comfortable. Most people grow up being taught what they are "supposed" to be doing. Many of these lessons are taught to them through the media, their family, and the community. We covered this briefly in Chapter 7 in discussing Massey's theory on how our values are shaped over time. People learn growing up that other people value certain activities, and doing those activities garners respect and acknowledgment.

Everyone likes to be acknowledged, so we become programmed to live in a way that pleases others. It can actually become automatic behavior, rather than a conscious decision. Instead of stopping to think about whether you like spending all day watching television, you might do it without thinking, because that's what your friends and family do. Or maybe you still live in the town you grew up in because that's what everyone in the community does, which made you never consider moving elsewhere.

While having your values influenced by those around you is normal, if it's at the expense of your true values and core desires in life, there is a problem. If your actions are a reflection of what the people around you want and not necessarily what you want, you are caught up in the minors. If you're following someone else's vision for your life, it doesn't matter how good or bad the vision is. The point is, the vision is not yours.

The good news is that we can get you out of the minors quickly. The first step is being honest and taking time to see if the values you are using as a guide in your day-to-day life are the ones that you have taken time to consciously choose or if they are a reflection of what someone else or society told you.

This reminds me of a quote attributed to George Bernard Shaw: "Life isn't about finding yourself; it is about creating yourself." You either allow society, friends, or family to create your life for you while you follow along, or you step up and decide to design the life of your dreams and make it happen!

Getting Bogged Down by Busy Work

Another factor that will get you stuck in the minors is if you're caught up in the daily hustle of life and letting the majors slip away from your focus. What does this mean? It's simple. It's when people get so caught up in everything they have to get done that they lose track of what is most important. An example of this would be a typical daily to-do list:

- Do the laundry.

- Pick up the kids.

- Get to the meeting.

- Finish the paperwork.

- Make dinner.

Goals are not the same as to do list

There are so many tasks to be done that we feel productive just making it through them all. However, motion doesn't guarantee progress. Just because we're getting work done doesn't mean we are getting the right work done. To-do lists can be like busy work, distracting us from the majors. Don't get me wrong. I'm not telling you to leave your kids across town and let them walk home! I'm saying that sometimes the items that get priority on a to-do list are not the majors, and time could be better spent on something else. There are plenty of ways to overcome this challenge. A simple example would be starting to carpool with another parent and alternating driving duty to save a little time. This could allow you to spend those extra moments doing something that would bring you closer to your Ideal Day vision. Try to focus your attention on tasks that lead to progress in your life. Being busy for the sake of being busy has the minors written all over it. Make sure you keep an eye out for those pitfalls.

If you find that you are either allowing someone else's values to guide your life or are just caught up in the daily hustle, I want to share with you a few things you can do to get yourself out of the minors and back on track to living your Ideal Day vision.

Limitations of the Mind

Often, people hold limiting beliefs about what they can accomplish in life, and those beliefs are what hold them back. Limiting beliefs can be about anything, but the basis is typically something along the lines of "I'm not smart enough/talented enough/young enough/old enough." When people hold thoughts like this, even in the back of their minds, it will keep them from going after their goals with the confidence and determination necessary for success.

In order to push past our limiting beliefs, it helps to recognize where they originated. We've already discussed how children and young adults are especially impressionable. Many of the limiting beliefs adults hold are a result of the experiences they had years earlier in life. Sometimes people were directly told they weren't good enough, but other times limiting beliefs are the result of another person's values being forced onto people. For example, there is a huge number of people raised around the world by parents who said, "If you live under this roof, you will follow my rules." There's a good chance you heard your mother, father, or whoever was in charge of your household say this to you when you were a kid. Children grow up following their family's rules, and often their family's value system becomes engrained into their minds as well. If parents or family members think challenging the status quo in life is dangerous and stupid, it's natural that their children will grow up with those limiting beliefs as well.

Although sometimes acquiring your family's belief system is less than ideal, it isn't a result of bad intentions. The reason parents and caretakers have so many rules is that they want their children to grow up safe and well positioned for future success. Traditional ideas for what creates a solid foundation for success have been fairly narrow in past generations, and they might not have changed much over the years, depending on the culture or individual family. Most expectations revolve around going to school, getting a steady job, and becoming a productive adult in society. When people believe specific actions are the only way to lead a good life, they will do all they can to make sure their loved ones follow that specific action plan. Anything outside of that plan is out of their comfort zones. While they know other options are available, it's hard to picture them being good options, because they are different from what these people have chosen for themselves. If that sounds familiar to you, maybe you can see how your family was never trying to limit your growth or success; they were just trying to protect you.

Unfortunately, these limiting beliefs can influence your life in a way that doesn't truly make you happy. Maybe you played it safe and did what was expected of you, but you don't love your daily life. What's worse is when people play it safe, and it turns around to bite them in the end. For example, in recent years a lot of jobs that used to be considered stable are no longer reliable in the long run. People used to put in their time even if they hated the work, because in the end they would be rewarded for their years of service, which made it all worth it. When that's no longer the case, staying in a job you aren't passionate about no longer seems like the safe or smart choice.

Overcoming Limiting Beliefs

When you recognize that you have limiting beliefs that are keeping you stuck in the minors, you have two options.

The first option is to change the story you keep telling yourself. Come up with a new story that supports you and helps you make progress and feel good about where you are and what you are doing. When you change your story, you will open the door to break out of your comfort zone and start changing your life.

The second option is to go out and find a way to change the results you are currently achieving in your life. Once you are able to change the real-world results, in turn, those results will crush that old limiting belief. This will require hard work, focus, and determination. If you are willing to put in the time and effort, you can quickly get out of the minors and create powerful results in your life and business.

When you took the time to design your Ideal Day vision in Chapter 1, how did the vision you had for your life make you feel? Did you feel lukewarm and bored? Or was your life filled with passion, adventure, and excitement as you challenged yourself to grow and give even more of who you are to the world? Did the events leading up to that day show you had limiting beliefs, so you followed a path that people expected you to take? Or did you challenge the status quo and do something out of the ordinary to achieve those results? Chances are good that you took a path less traveled. Keep this in mind when you go through challenging times. Some people settle for the status quo because they have not taken the time to discover what else is available, or they are too afraid to step outside of their comfort zones to get the results they dream of. Challenging the status quo can be scary at first, but it's worth it. One positive thing about having fewer "safe" choices in the professional world is that it becomes easier to follow your passion!

One of the greatest gifts you can give to future generations is to teach the value of independence and following dreams. It encourages young people to dive deep within themselves and discover their true passions in life. It inspires a vision that anything is possible—especially making the world a better place. When young people grow up with confidence, it ultimately impacts innovation and creativity for coming up with new ways to approach problems that the world faces and empowers them to tackle issues head-on.

LIVE IT CHALLENGE

Even if you believe that you were made to do amazing things on this planet and have taken the time to prepare yourself by gathering all of the tools and strategies, you can still get stuck in the minors. What gets you stuck is not a lack of knowledge; it is a lack of applying that knowledge and taking the actions to get the results you are after. Here is a quick exercise to help get you back on track.

Identify a limiting story that is holding you back.

1. If you are currently stuck in the minors, what is the story you are telling yourself about why you are not getting the results you desire or deserve?

2. How is that story preventing you from getting the results you are after? How is it keeping you from living your Ideal Day vision?

3. What can you do today to challenge that story or to change the results that are currently showing up in your day-to-day life?

Learned Helplessness

Like limitations of the mind, learned helplessness can cause you to get stuck in the minors for good. The Oxford Dictionary defines learned helplessness as a condition in which a person suffers from a sense of powerlessness, arising from a traumatic event or persistent failure to succeed. Oxford also mentions that this condition is thought to be one of the underlying causes of depression.[2] Learned helplessness generally occurs when people feel that no matter what they do, they are always stuck in the same painful situation. Instead of believing there might be a different outcome if they keep trying, people can sometimes get stuck in a rut thinking they are doomed for failure. As a result, they stop trying, and they miss out on everything they could have accomplished. While trying something and having it not work out can be painful, it's even worse to give up and miss out on what you really want. When that happens, trust me, you will be stuck in the minors for good.

Successful people are sometimes seen as lucky; they were either born with an innate skill set that sets them apart, or they were in the right place at the right time to make their dreams come true. In reality, most successful people aren't any luckier than anyone else. What does set them apart is their determination. When they fail, they keep trying. Repeatedly. They don't think they are helpless in shaping their future, even when the world knocks them down. We don't usually hear about these challenging times in the lives of successful people, however. We admire them when they reach their goals, but we didn't see what it took them to get there.

J. K. Rowling is a great example of this. She is famous for authoring the Harry Potter book series, the bestselling book series in history, which has sold 400 million copies worldwide.[3] Today, the world agrees that Rowling is a prolific author, but many people might not know that she had a hard time getting people to believe in her talent and her story. The fact that the world knows Harry Potter at all is a testament to Rowling in itself; she was turned down by twelve publishers before one finally believed in her and the Harry Potter fantasy world.[4]

Being turned down twelve times in a row can feel like a lot! Think about being turned down twelve times in a row by different people when asking them out on a date, interviewing for a job, or trying out for a team. Many people would quit long before being told no that many times.

Why didn't Rowling quit? She had a lot of reasons to believe her big dream wouldn't come true. She was going through a hard time when other aspects of her life seemed to be falling apart. Her mother had died, she had gotten divorced, and she and her daughter were living in poverty, on the verge of being homeless. Instead of feeling helpless, as if her future were out of her control, she directed all of her energy toward finishing the only thing that mattered to her—the first Harry Potter book. She tapped into her Emotional Rocket Fuel and stayed focused on her biggest dream. Instead of settling for a career she didn't care about, she was determined to do what she wanted most.

How many people out there could have been like Rowling but stopped after being rejected a few times? Or maybe threw in the towel after ten or eleven times and just barely missed living their dream? A lot. And I'm not just talking about writing books here. This is true for all goals.

If you think you're helpless, you will be helpless. If you believe you can do something, you give yourself a fighting chance. If you find yourself stuck in the minors and/or in a moment of learned helplessness, here are a few things you can do to immediately get yourself unstuck and back on track.

How to Get Unstuck

The first step to getting out of the minors is to make a decision to become conscious of your current values. Not what you tell yourself you value most, or what you tell those around you that you value, but what you *actually value* in your daily life. When was the last time you consciously identified and wrote down your current values? For most people, the answer is never. I want you to be one of the few people who is living life with awareness and intention, and this exercise will help show you how.

In order to do this, let's take a moment to assess how you're spending your time. There are 168 hours in one week. Most people spend roughly 49 to 56 hours sleeping per week (7 to 8 hours per night). That leaves 112 to 119 waking hours left per week.

How do you spend that time?

LIVE IT CHALLENGE

- Take out your notebook and pen, and write down your average schedule for one week.

- Next, determine how much time you are spending per week on various activities. For example, maybe you spend three hours watching TV each night, which adds up to twenty-one hours per week. If it bugs you to write that down, it's OK. Being honest is the first step toward making a change in your life.

- Finally, group your activities into categories, such as work, fitness, or family, to determine how you are investing your time. Tally up the hours and put the categories in ranking order from where you spend the most time to the least.

As you may remember, in the last chapter you took the time to identify the things in life you value most and the order of importance of those things. How does that list compare to how you are actually spending your time? For most people, these lists look pretty different. In the exercise in the last chapter, you might have listed your top values as family, God, health, being a good person, and giving back. In your daily life, those values could be allotted a disproportionately small amount of time compared to other activities (like your day job) that didn't even make your list of values.

The most precious resource we have in life is our time. Although we can say we value certain aspects of life, when we invest our most precious resource in other ways, there is a conflict. If you aren't already living your ideal day every single day, this discrepancy in how you spend your time is likely a key reason. If while going through this exercise you noticed a difference between what you value and your day-to-day life, you need to shift your focus to making progress in the majors of life, immediately.

Most people find that their work takes up the largest portion of their weekly schedule (besides sleep). I'd like you to take a serious look at this part of your life. Sometimes people don't include work on their list of top values because they think other aspects should come first. However, if you are putting a large portion of your time and effort into work, it is currently a top value for you. Maybe you are thinking about it as success or personal achievement rather than work. There is nothing wrong with valuing work, but it's important to be honest with yourself about whether it truly is a core value and how it compares to your other values. Does your work encompass other values you listed in the previous chapter, such as helping others or constantly learning new things? If so, you can live your values while working, which is a great fit for your life. If work doesn't allow you to experience your true values, it can be seen as a burden that is taking up your most precious resource without giving you the proper return on that investment. While it may be difficult to cut back working hours because you need to earn a living and support your family, know that when you spend a lot of time working, you will need to become even better at budgeting the rest of your time to spend it on actions that align with your values.

Your Ideal Day vision is another key tool you can use to get out of the rut you're currently stuck in. Also make sure to set up your Live It List, challenge yourself to get specific on a timeline, and take immediate action to turn those to-do items into reality. These steps should help you break free of the minors and build momentum toward turning your Ideal Day vision into reality.

Stay Aware

As you work to transition out of the minors and stay out of them for good, it's likely that you will experience dissonance from the world around you. Some people won't approve of your choices or priorities, or understand your goals. I experienced this myself, and many of my clients have as well. When people aren't as supportive as you would like, it can be harder to stay on the right path to meet your goals. However, it is essential to understand that many people struggle to see the world through anyone else's eyes.

There are different levels of awareness in life, and these levels are a key influence on how people interpret the world around them. Learning to be conscious of other people's models of the world is a massive step in staying out of the minors for good. Let me give you a simple scale to help you better understand the four levels of awareness.

Level 1—Self—People in the first level of awareness care about themselves and getting their own needs met. They do not realize that others have a different point of view, or they automatically think a different point of view is wrong. Swiss developmental psychologist and philosopher Jean Piaget referred to this as egocentrism. Piaget identified this life stage during his knowledge studies with children, as it typically occurs between two to seven years old, but can vary greatly depending on the person. Adults who are stuck in level 1 are in the same situation as a child, not realizing that others have a different set of values or beliefs about the world around them.

Level 2—Community—When people advance to level 2 on the awareness scale, they realize other viewpoints exist in the world, but the only viewpoints they recognize or agree with are those that match their community of friends, family members, churchgoers, or neighbors. People in this life stage put their community's needs first and have great difficulty connecting deeply with anyone outside of that community. When they encounter people who view life through a different lens, they can't relate.

Level 3—Global—People who advance to this level of awareness understand there is an abundance of viewpoints, values, and belief systems in the world. They no longer think of values as right or wrong, but instead see the value in diversity. This is a giant leap forward from level 2. In fact, many people in the world never advance to this level of awareness.

Level 4—Spiritual—This is the highest level of awareness, when people appreciate other viewpoints and attempt to step in and experience others' models of the world. When people reach this level, they believe that we all are connected as one universal energy. This level of awareness goes a step beyond the last level, because in addition to recognizing that people are different, those at level 4 appreciate that difference. Instead of feeling separated from people because of differences, at this level, people see perfection in the world around them just how it is. They allow life to unfold naturally around them, and as it does, they soak in the perfection of the moment. When they cross paths with someone who has a radically different set of values or beliefs, they enjoy the experience in the moment and then move on to the next opportunity that life sends their way. People with this level of awareness feel connected to the whole world around them, including animals, nature, and the earth.[5]

Give It (and When Not to Give It)

As you work to dig your way out of the minors and increase your level of awareness, keep your eye out for a common pitfall. You might find yourself relating better to people who are also becoming more aware of the vast world around them. On the other hand, longtime relationships you've had with people who are lower or stagnant on the awareness spectrum might start to feel strained. You are making progress growing and evolving as a person, and if they aren't evolving as well, it can feel like you're growing apart. It's natural to want to share the growth experience with the people you care about, and it can be frustrating when that doesn't work out.

I experienced this when I got back from Uganda. I believed the purpose of my life was to give back, do good things in the world, and focus on helping others. I was on a mission to spread this message and get everyone to align with *my* personal values and vision for life. My heart was in the right place, but I was pushing my viewpoints on other people, whether they liked it or not.

This is exactly what you want to avoid! If you have ever had family members or friends who act like this, you know it becomes very uncomfortable at times to be around them. They are constantly lecturing you on your health, your diet, how you should be living your life, how you raise your children, how you run your business, and so on. Not only are people like that annoying, but their lecturing at you doesn't make an impact if you aren't interested in what they have to say.

It is important to realize that not all people want to change their lives, and not everyone feels ready to do so. This is not right, wrong, good, or bad; it just is. Trying to force change on others can make them feel like you are looking down on them, like they aren't good enough. Belittling people is a behavior that is related to a lower level of awareness; it's not done by someone who is spiritually, or even globally, aware. As you improve your life, make sure you don't start to look down your nose at people who are fine with their lives just as they are. Focus on appreciating people for who they are today.

Instead of trying to push change on people who aren't ready to change, the best thing you can do is lead by example. When people show an interest in what you're doing, it opens a dialogue to share your experiences. By talking about focusing on the majors in life and staying true to your values, you will inspire others to do the same.

Pushing my viewpoints on my friends and family wasn't well received when I first returned from Uganda. I learned how much more effective it is to lead by example and help people who want my help. I now make sure the advice I give people is tailored to their own values and goals, instead of my own.

The greatest leaders on earth are servants to their people's needs, rather than their own needs. They respect what other people value most in life and do their absolute best to help them make progress and reach their goals. If you really want to Give it, focus on servant leadership. You will be amazed at how many people you can inspire. The greatest mark of a leader is not how many people follow, but how many leaders he or she creates.

LIVE IT CHALLENGE

- Which level of awareness do you spend the majority of your time on?

- How would life be different if you were able to live consistently at level 4 on the awareness scale?

- What has to happen for you to make the transition to level 4?

- What can you do to remind yourself to respect the values of others around you versus trying to get them to adhere to your personal values?

CHAPTER 9:

FINDING THE TRUE YOU

"The privilege of a lifetime is to become who you truly are."
—*attributed to Carl Jung*

On your journey out of the minors, you may have a moment when you realize that you were stuck there because you were living an inauthentic life, disconnected from who you are at the core. You were making choices, either consciously or subconsciously, to get love, approval, respect, or appreciation from a specific person or the world around you. Instead of being your authentic self, you ended up bending, twisting, and acting in ways you hoped would earn approval from those around you.

As human beings, we crave a sense of belonging. We want people to like us, whether we admit it or not. Because of this, it's easy to develop different personas, versions of ourselves that come out depending on the people we are around at the time. We become a chameleon, constantly shifting to encompass what we think people want us to be at the moment, whether it's at work or school, spending time with our friends, or meeting someone new. People have a tendency to adapt to their environment to fit in. In fact, some even say we are hardwired to do this, since our ancestors depended on being a part of a social group for survival. Although times have changed, the emotional need for love and belonging is still a defining human trait. It's important to recognize this as part of the journey in finding your authentic self at the core.

While bending to fit in may help you feel acceptance in that moment, it isn't good for your long-term well-being. You will never be able to live your ideal life if you are shaping it around what other people want. What makes other people happy will not necessarily make you happy. What is most important to them might not truly matter to you at all. It is essential to realize this, or you are bound to find yourself spinning your wheels and losing focus on how to best make progress in your life.

Luckily for us, individuality has become more accepted than in past years. People no longer have to fit a specific mold to feel like they are a part of something, as diversity has become a priority in schools, the workplace, and social circles. There are campaigns that teach young children that it is wrong to bully people who are different. We have seen the gay rights movement gain strength and support around the United States, and we have our first African American president. Times have changed dramatically in just a few generations, because people no longer accept the old way of doing things. The modern approach to life is to celebrate people for who they are—there's no longer a need to put on a facade to fit in.

This chapter is focused on helping you discover (or rediscover) the authentic you! You must uncover and step into the true and authentic you if want to experience a full life.

Becoming your authentic self sounds easy, but it can actually be quite complex. Thinking back to Massey's theory, sometimes ideas you've held for a long time about the type of person you should be feel like they are your own ideas, but they were actually sparked by the people around you. Those ideas can become so engrained over the years that it takes some soul-searching to sift through them and determine which ideas you agree with and which you could do without.

On my twenty-sixth birthday, I attended a course produced by Oneness University and Robbins Research International. The group was led by monks from India who were in Fiji teaching a course on building self-awareness. Participants were taken through exercises that ultimately help create oneness in everyone and everything. I was extremely excited to participate in this class and curious about what the effects would be.

A major component of the course was taught by my father. He walked us through a process focused on finding our true, authentic selves. During this exercise, I realized that much of what I was doing at that point in my life was not true or authentic to me. Somehow, I had gotten off track. My choices weren't making me happy or helping me build the life I ultimately desired. In that moment, I realized I was making those choices not for me, but for my father. I was doing things in search of his approval, respect, love, and acceptance. It was an ironic yet beautiful moment, learning from my father that I needed to reshape my values to better align with who I was, instead of who I thought he wanted me to be.

Before you can fully experience love and respect from other people, you have to love and respect yourself. This only comes when you are being *the real you*. If you constantly try to be the person you think you need to be in order to get people's love, others will never have the chance to actually love *you*! They can share their love with you, but you will never feel it, because in that moment, they are not sharing their love with the true, authentic you; they are sharing it with the person you are pretending to be.

Discovering Your Authentic Self

When you can find a way to love your real self and just be the person you naturally are when you are not worried about what other people think, your authentic self will shine through. The moment you are able to love, appreciate, and accept the true, authentic you is the moment you set yourself free once and for all. You will become empowered to turn your Ideal Day vision into reality without ever worrying or second-guessing yourself. You will be able to tap into what is referred to as your inner guide, your heart, and your gut instincts. By connecting to the core of who you are and becoming more aware of what your heart wants, making decisions and knowing what is right for you is much easier.

The Authentic You Exercise

I would like to walk you through my version of the exercise that I went through during the Oneness course. This concept is often used by licensed psychotherapists to help clients uncover what is holding them back. It has proven to be highly effective in helping people discover—or rediscover—who they are at their core. We will take a look at these questions to ultimately make sure your vision is on track and aligned with your true self.

There are six important questions in this process. Take out your notebook and pen to record your answers.

Question 1: From whom did you want love, approval, or acceptance the most when you were growing up? To be clear, it's not whom you received positive reinforcement from the most; it's whom you wanted or desired it from the most.

I remember for me, it was my grandmother on my mom's side and my father. My mom gave me endless amounts of positive reinforcement, so it wasn't something I yearned for as much. In my perception, my dad and my grandma had rules of who I had to be to earn their love, respect, acceptance, and approval, which made me crave those things even more.

From whom did you want love, approval, acceptance, and attention the most?

Question 2: Who did you think you had to be in order to receive this positive reinforcement?

For me, this was simple. I had to be, a hardworking, determined, focused, good boy. I had to be respectful, dressed properly with my hair combed and shirt tucked in. I had to be a caring, loving, giving person, and the list goes on and on.

I remember when I first shared this perception with my dad. We were on a long plane ride together, heading out on a father-son adventure trip to see the silverback gorillas in Rwanda. He asked me about my experience with this exercise, and he was especially surprised to hear that I thought he cared about me being dressed "properly" at all times. He asked what could have given me that impression. I told him about the time we had taken family photos when I was about twelve years old, and my stepmom pulled me aside. She said my dad would be very disappointed if my shirt was untucked and my hair wasn't combed. She was referring to my appearance just for the photo, but apparently I thought she was talking about how I dressed in general. That one comment left a lasting impression on what I thought my dad wanted me to be, and it wasn't even based on something he particularly cared about. After learning this, it seemed silly that I had let a single comment determine how I felt about getting my dad's love and approval, but I realized how often this must happen to people.

Does this spark any memories for you? Did a family member or friend ever say something in passing that has stayed with you since then and shaped your perception of the person you think you have to be to get love, respect, acceptance, or approval? If you are challenged by this question, just think back to all of the actions that you were positively reinforced for doing. If you were to ask the people you listed in question 1 what they respect most about you, what would they say?

Question 3: Who did you think you could never be, or you would lose these people's positive reinforcement? Sometimes the answer to this is the reciprocal belief of question 2, but sometimes people focus on specific qualities.

I thought I could never be sloppy, disrespectful, mean, rude, angry, aggressive, or lazy. I thought if I were that type of person I would lose my grandmother's and my father's approval, love, and respect. One reason for this belief is that I could see how people in my family felt about others who they thought embodied those qualities. For example, many of them prided themselves in being hardworking. As a result, I assumed my family wouldn't be pleased with me if I were a lazy person.

Who did you think you could never be or you would lose the positive reinforcement from the people you wanted it from most?

Question 4: Who are you today? Out of everything you listed earlier, which traits are still part of how you would describe yourself now?

When I first did this exercise, I was a pretty clear reflection of those answers I gave to the previous questions on who I thought I had to be. I was well put together, nice, genuine, giving, and caring. I did my best to never be lazy, and I always worked my hardest and gave my all to everyone around me.

I shared this exercise with my mom a few years back. When we got to this question, she started crying. I felt horrible! I wasn't sure what made her so upset, but I knew the question struck a nerve. She told me that she realized she had been trying to be the person she thought she had to be to earn her father's love and respect, and she had been living that way for forty-six years. She was the firstborn, and for the first few years, her dad did everything with her, including going fishing and playing sports. Then her brother was born, and she felt like she was kicked to the curb, because her dad wanted to do everything with him. For years and years she was working hard, always trying to show or prove that she was tough enough, strong enough, and worthy of his respect. She said she realized in that moment that she had been allowing her desire to please her dad guide her whole life.

Who are you today? What are all of the traits you would use to best describe how you live your current day-to-day life?

Question 5: What would you have to add or completely remove from this list of who you are today to be the true, authentic you—to get back to who you are at your core and be the person who is capable of turning your Ideal Day vision into reality?

Upon self-reflection, I saw that my outward image was the good, caring, nice, sweet person that I described on the list of who I was today. But I wasn't being myself. I still wanted to be a nice person, but I didn't feel like that was the defining part of my true personality. I identified with so many other attributes more than just being nice. At heart, I was adventurous, determined, passionate, wild, fun, and spontaneous. I had repressed those parts of myself for so long because I thought these aspects of my personality would garner disapproval. To be the authentic me, I would have to bring those attributes to life.

What do you have to add to or completely remove from your list to be your true, authentic you—the person who is capable of turning your Ideal Day vision into reality?

Question 6: What would you need more or less of on this list to be the true, authentic you? Sometimes your current self has some aspects of your authentic self, but some traits are magnified and some are downplayed. If there's anything you can identify that you need less or more of to become more authentic, write those traits down and put a plus or minus sign next to it.

For me, I needed to focus less on being nice and polite. Of course I didn't want to totally eliminate those personality traits, but I needed to downplay them, because they were compromising my authentic self—the person who chooses adventure over playing it safe to please others.

Making the Shift Happen from the Old You to the Authentic You

Now that you have thought about your answers to these six questions, it should be easy to see whether the person you are today is a reflection of your true self or of the desire to please others. If you have discovered areas that don't align, you understand what needs to change to become more authentic.

When I first realized I had to make a shift in my life, the thought was a little scary. I felt the risk of making a change in who I was, and I worried about repercussions. Taking it a step further and following through with what I needed to do, rather than just thinking about it, was a big deal. I knew I needed to break free of old patterns, but I was worried about what people would think of me. As you start to make the shift to your authentic self, it's likely you will feel the same way.

Before we move forward, let's talk about the idea of change. It is something that can make people uncomfortable, even when they aren't the person who is changing! When we already love people just the way they are, we can be afraid of losing that love and relationship if they change. That's why people sometimes see change as a negative thing. You've probably heard people say, "Oh, he's changed," their tone showing the disdain they feel. Comments like this make it seem as if people should never change; we should all just keep on living exactly how we are for the rest of our lives.

The problem with this perspective is that it doesn't accept personal growth. Most people have not reached their full potential, especially when they still have years of life experience ahead of them. I grew up being taught that everything in life is either growing or dying. If you take a fruit tree, for example, it starts as a seed and eventually grows into a tree. As a tree it continues to grow and produce fruit. Eventually, it gets to a point where it no longer produces fruit, and it stops growing. At the very moment the tree stops growing, it actually begins to die. Sometimes the outside of the tree looks strong, yet the inside is slowly rotting away. The same goes for people. Just like a tree, if you aren't making progress and growing, you are dying.

In addition to accepting change as a natural human process, we need to do another check on personal values. Based on my experience, when people take time to identify their true authentic self, their personal values begin to shift. Let's take some time to evaluate and potentially realign the values you discovered in Chapter 7. Make sure your values represent the authentic you. If you are going to turn your dream life into your day-to-day life, you can no longer allow society, friends, family, and the world around you to shape your personal values. You have to take charge of your life by using your Ideal Day vision, your Live It List, and all the other tools we have covered thus far in the book to be your guide in establishing your true personal values.

Case Study

Let me introduce you to a good friend named Alex and share how this exercise helped him realize the life he was living wasn't authentic and would never lead him to his Ideal Day vision, and what steps he took to get his life on the right track.

Alex grew up in Chicago's South Side. As you may know, neighborhoods in the South Side are some of the most dangerous places in the United States, with violent crime rates soaring high above the national average. Two of Alex's closest friends were murdered before they were twenty-one years old. Living in a dangerous area helped shape Alex's outlook and life plan.

Growing up, he had always yearned for his father's respect and love. To give you some history, his father was one of twelve children who grew up as hardworking sharecroppers in Mississippi. They had to do exactly what they needed to do in order to survive and put food on the table. This experience shaped Alex's father's life and the way he parented Alex. As a result, Alex thought he had to share the same priorities as his father and live in the same ways that his father did in order to earn his love and respect. He always felt that he needed to grow up to be a respectable black man, which meant he needed to get a good job, make a lot of money, and prove to the world that he had "made it."

So what did he do? As a young man, he worked incredibly hard in school, graduated, moved out of Chicago, and got a job at DreamWorks, where he became a go-to guy in the company. He was the good guy whom everyone could count on. When I met him, he was very proud of his accomplishments and focused on how he could achieve bigger and better results. That is why he joined us on our Rapid Results Retreat in December 2013. However, he went through the Authentic You process and sure enough, it became a turning point in his life and career.

Alex discovered that the life he had built for himself was a result of his desire to show to his father and the world that he had made it as a successful and respectable black man. Although his father and community in Chicago had never sat him down and explicitly said this was the way he needed to be, Alex had an understanding of what would be impressive to people and what would earn his father's respect. He subconsciously shaped his life to please others, instead of himself. The exercise was an awakening, and he made a decision to finally allow his heart to lead instead of his head.

As he went through this process, he noticed that some of the aspects of his life that were once most important to him no longer seemed to matter. For example, when he came on the retreat, he was focused on being successful, number one in everything he did, and upholding a clean-cut image. In focusing on these aspects of his life and image, he neglected parts of his true personality. He started to realize how much he truly cares about growth, love, spirituality, and contribution, and how absent those things were from his life. His values started to naturally realign themselves when he became real and authentic instead of trying to be the man he thought he was supposed to be.

Alex's original values:

- Success

- Perfection

- Clean-cut appearance

- Being number one in everything he did

Alex's new values:

- Personal growth

- Love

- Spirituality

- Contribution

- Success

This shift affected Alex's life dramatically, which is shown by how his day-to-day reality has changed since the retreat. He transitioned out of the corporate world to pursue a career that he could be more passionate about—helping young people discover their true calling in the world and make a plan for living their passion. In transition, he spent a few months traveling around Europe then stayed in the United Kingdom for another few months working directly with college students. He is now living in Australia and building his business inspiring young people around the globe to follow their dreams right after they graduate, instead of waiting until later in life like he did. He shared with me that he has never felt so alive, free, passionate, and full in his entire life. He feels that he is finally connected to his true calling and purpose in life.

I am excited for you to be able to feel the same—and for those of you who are already aligned with your mission and purpose in life to be able to amplify it at a whole new level!

LIVE IT CHALLENGE

Take some time to realign your values to represent your true, authentic nature.

Step 1—Go through each one of your values and ask yourself, "Is this authentically me or an old representation of who I thought I needed to be?"

Step 2—If a value is the true, authentic you, keep it! If it is the old representation of you, either remove it completely from the list or push it further down your priorities.

For example, after Alex went through the Authentic You process, he still valued success, but not as much as love, God, or contribution. Success went from number one to number five on his second list because he still valued it, but not as much.

Step 3—Add any new values that you feel are most important in making up the true, authentic you.

Step 4—Compare each value like we did in Chapter 7 to make sure all the values are in the order that serves you best.

For most people reading this chapter, it will be an eye-opening experience. A variety of emotions may unveil themselves along the journey—everything from disbelief, sadness, and feeling conflicted, all the way to joy, bliss, and freedom.

LIVE IT CHALLENGE
If you have realigned your values, make sure they stick.

- Review your new values daily for the next month.

- Ask yourself whether you are taking actions that reflect your new values. If not, make plans to do things that are a better match for living your authentic life.

- Don't forget that change is a natural part of living authentically. Make sure you do the Authentic You exercise every few years.

The ball is in your court to make the changes necessary for living an authentic life.

CHAPTER 10:

HARNESSING YOUR MENTAL STRENGTH

When you discover (or rediscover) your authentic self and start heading in a new direction, sometimes it can feel like you're taking a step backward. You may be starting at the beginning of a new endeavor and rebuilding from the ground up. This is a time when you need to harness your mental strength more than ever.

I found this out through personal experience. After finishing up two years on the road as an outside sales representative and realizing that the only reason I was doing that job was to try to get the approval, love, and respect I wanted from my father, I decided to make a transition and follow my Ideal Day vision. I was ready to go out and live my purpose and mission of inspiring people to learn, live, and give all that they are humanly capable of to reach their full potential. I decided not to settle any longer for doing the things I thought I was supposed to be doing to get the appreciation, respect, and love from certain people in my life.

I quit the outside sales job and moved back to my hometown of San Diego. At the time, I didn't have another job lined up, and I wasn't sure how I would be able to pay my bills. All I knew was that in order to move forward I had to make a change immediately, and somehow it would all work out in the end. My life became filled with uncertainty, and there was no way around that. I had to get comfortable venturing into the unknown if I wanted a real chance at improving my life.

I booked my flight and packed my bags, excited about the journey ahead of me. In fact, I was so excited to be starting a new chapter in my life that I had overlooked a crucial element until the last minute—finding a place to live! Surely I could stay at a hotel or at a friend's house until I found a long-term solution. Before taking off, I sent a text to a handful of friends asking if they knew of a place for rent or if they were looking for a roommate. It was a Thursday night, which I realized might not be ideal for dropping in on someone who has to work or go to school the next morning, but it was a little late to plan ahead.

Upon landing, which was around ten thirty at night, I had received one text back from a good friend saying she had two rooms for rent at her house. I texted her back and asked if I could come see the rooms. She said sure and asked when I could stop by. Since her place was pretty close to the airport, I jumped in a rental car and told her I would be there in a few minutes. I'm sure she was wondering what I was up to, since I was coming to see a room at eleven on a Thursday night. When I arrived, she gave me a quick tour of the house and showed me the rooms that were available. Only one of the rooms was available that night because the other one still had someone living in it through the weekend. The room that was available immediately was the front den of the house, which didn't even have a real door separating it from the living room. It was far from my dream living situation, but I realized I wasn't in a position to be picky. I told my friend the room was great and I would like to rent it. She asked when I would like to move in, and I'll never forget the look on her face when I said, "I'll go get my bags!"

I had been in San Diego for only an hour, and things were already falling into place. Embracing uncertainty even added a little more excitement to my journey. Now that I had found a place to live, the next day I set out to find a job. I had been doing some one-on-one coaching as a part-time job for the past five years, and I loved it. I wanted to continue doing that, but it wasn't enough hours per week to make a living. I had to find something else that would keep me afloat while I figured out exactly how I was going to turn my Ideal Day vision into reality.

Even though I had made the decision to dig myself out of the minors, I knew the transformation to living a better life would be a process, rather than an overnight change to perfection. There would be the inevitable stepping stones along the way, and as long as I was making progress that is what mattered. I already felt better just from doing something different, and that added Emotional Rocket Fuel to my fire. Now that the wheels were in motion, all I had to do was put together a plan for building a business that would reflect my authentic values. During this process, there were bound to be more challenging times, especially since at that point, I wasn't looking for the perfect long-term job. I just needed to pay my bills and get health insurance.

I ended up finding not one, but three part-time jobs that together would equal full-time hours and get me the health insurance I needed. I was ready to hustle and rebuild a financial foundation, working these jobs along with coaching and focusing on my own business. One of my new jobs was working in a warehouse, something I had never particularly wanted to do, but I was ready to make the best of it. The first few days were actually fun. I learned how to drive the forklift, and I got satisfaction from helping organize shipments of various products.

Unfortunately, having fun at the warehouse didn't last very long. During a team meeting one day, we were told there was an old flyer that needed to be removed from fifteen hundred packages that day and replaced with a new one. I looked over at three pallets of boxes piled high and filled with all of these programs. I remember thinking, "Uh oh, this looks like a lot of work." It certainly was. I'll never forget that day because it consisted of the following:

- Open the big box.

- Pull out a little box.

- Open the little box.

- Pull out the program.

- Unzip the program.

- Pull out the workbook.

- Flip to the back.

- Pull out the old page.

- Put in the new page.

- Close the workbook.

- Put it back in the program.

- Zip it shut.

- Put it back in the little box.

- Close the little box.

- Put it back in the big box.

- Repeat fifteen hundred times!

I'll never forget getting to around five hundred flyers and becoming frustrated, getting to a thousand and being ready to pop, and finally getting to fifteen hundred and repeating to myself, "I will never do this again!" I had hit my mental, emotional, and physical threshold—I hated what I was doing so much that it turned into Emotional Rocket Fuel for doing whatever it took to turn my dream life into my real life. I knew what it would take to fall in love with the process, but this time I decided to use it as my fuel to inspire action and change instead. There was no way I would end up living a life where I unpacked and repacked boxes all day. I would go crazy.

That night after work I went home and sat in my new room, a.k.a. the front den. I wanted to shut the door and have some privacy, but of course there was no door, only two curtains that didn't even match. I looked around at the few pieces of cheap furniture and a couple of suitcases' worth of clothes and possessions, and I thought about how much it looked like a room belonging to a college student. I had graduated a few years earlier and had hoped to upgrade my living situation by this point in my life, but this most recent move was definitely a downgrade. The day I had in the warehouse felt like a downgrade as well. For a moment, I felt a twinge of doubt about the choices I had just made. I knew I was taking the action necessary to move forward, but it was hard to ignore that I had embarked on an uphill battle. Maybe I had underestimated the challenge in front of me.

I decided I needed to make as much progress as I could, as quickly as I could, to keep up my excitement and momentum. Above all, I couldn't lose my motivation to go after what I truly wanted. That night, I wrote down every single tool I could use and every single action I could take to stay focused and push forward to reach my goals. I was at a place in my life where having mental strength would make more of a difference in my success than it ever had before.

In the coming weeks, I tried to create a lot of tools, exercises, and imagery techniques to build my motivation and harness my mental strength. Through trial and error, I found a handful that made a huge impact on my life. As you journey out of the minors and start to rebuild different areas of your life, these tools will help you maintain the mental fortitude you need for staying on track when the going gets tough.

Filling and Fueling

There's no saying what's in store for us on any given day, but one thing is certain—some days will be hard! Life will throw things at you that strike you off guard. They may be small inconveniences that test your patience, or they may be enough to make you question yourself and whether you are capable of success in the long run. The best thing you can do is face each day being your strongest self, so that the guaranteed hiccups in life don't crush your spirit or your confidence.

A good analogy of this is a soda can. If you took a soda can that was a quarter full and handed it to a small child, even though the child may be weak, they would easily be able to dent or even crush it. However, if that same can was 100 percent full and sealed, it would be much more difficult to dent or crush by squeezing it.

When the can is sealed, the pressure is pushing out, and it is more resistant to anything pushing into it.

Imagine you are that soda can when you go out to take on the world each day. Are you heading out mentally, emotionally, and physically a quarter full, or are you going out into the world 100 percent full with positive emotions sealed in and even pushing out to protect you? Your natural state of mind will make a huge difference in how you feel when life takes a swing at you and hits you with its best shot. You can either get dented or crushed immediately, or easily forge through any challenges that life sends your way.

Keep thinking about the imagery of the soda can throughout this chapter. The following exercises will show you how you can step out into the world being 100 percent full, day after day. Regardless of the goals you are after—if you want to get fit, lose some weight, start a business, or maximize your personal or professional results—these tools will be the foundation for pushing forward to get the results you desire and deserve. If you want to achieve amazing results in life, it all starts in your mind.

Add Automation to Your Motivation

I have to be honest; some days I wake up feeling fired up, passionate, excited, and ready to take on the world, but other days are a different story. I might feel as if a small army were needed to help motivate me, because I'm certainly not pumped up for the day, excited to get out there and make things happen, and I definitely don't feel like working out. Maybe you can relate to finding yourself in this position every now and then. I figured out a few super simple ways to spark my mental and emotional fuel on the days when I need a little extra support—like making a YouTube playlist of clips that motivate me, or an audio playlist of songs and audio clips that get me energized and excited about my day. You can also record your Ideal Day vision over music if you want and listen to it to create some Emotional Rocket Fuel for your day!

Vision Board

Like automating your motivation helps you get pumped audibly, a vision board helps you visualize your motivation. This tool helps you gather inspiring thoughts, ideas, quotes, and affirmations and put them all in one place you can visit regularly as a reminder of the most important elements and goals in your life.

You may be familiar with vision boards and already thinking about the types of images to include: a stack of cash, a fancy car, oceanfront property, and a perfect body. Not so fast. Martha Beck, a sociologist with a PhD from Harvard University and columnist at Oprah.com, says this type of vision board doesn't work.[1] The types of images people gravitate to for vision boards are usually a product of what our culture tells us is a mark of success, rather than what actually inspires us. The key to picking out the best images is thinking with your heart instead of your head. Flip through a magazine and notice when your heart starts thumping, your face suddenly has a big smile on it, or something catches your attention. If you aren't sure why you like an image and find it moving, that's OK. Listen to your instincts and allow them to guide you toward the images, thoughts, and ideas you will use to fill up your vision board. Cut out the images and attach them to a piece of cardboard, corkboard, or a stiff piece of paper.

From there, post it somewhere visible, but don't obsess over it. Beck believes in the power of letting go and allowing the intentions you've set in the world to work their magic. Seeing your vision board regularly instills what you care about most into your subconscious, which helps guide you toward success. This doesn't mean you don't have to put in any elbow grease; nothing is a substitute for taking action. Your vision board is simply a tool to help keep you mentally and emotionally engaged in your vision.

An effective way to modernize this process is to create a digital version of your vision board that you can add to the photo gallery of your smartphone, tablet, or computer and have with you everywhere you go. If you make it the background image, it serves as a constant reminder.

Mental Rehearsal

A tried-and-true method for improving performance comes from mental rehearsals. This is the act of envisioning exactly what you are about to do and focusing on how you will do it to the best of your ability. This is different from simply visualizing yourself doing well, where the perspective may be external, like watching a movie. While that type of positive thinking is helpful, mental rehearsal keeps the vision in your own perspective, like you are seeing it with your own two eyes, exactly as you imagine it happening in the future. Rehearsals also differ from visualization because they aren't abstract. Rehearsals make people think about a specific plan.

If you're skeptical about the effectiveness of mental rehearsals in improving performance, it's helpful to know how prevalent this technique is among athletes. Studies have shown that mental rehearsals do, in fact, improve psychomotor and sports performance. Many sports legends have used mental rehearsal, including Muhammad Ali. Ali mentally rehearsed every moment of upcoming fights in his head, including the fatigue he expected to feel in his legs, the sweat pouring off his body, the pain to his kidneys, the bruises on his face, the flash of the photographers, the exultant screams of the crowd, and even the moment when the referee lifts his arm in victory. By including mental rehearsals as part of his training regimen, he felt more prepared to execute his moves in the ring.

Now you may be thinking, "But I'm not an athlete. What does this have to do with helping me reach my goals?" The answer is simple. Athletes focus on personal performance, which is no different from what you need to focus on to achieve your Ideal Day vision. I have worked with clients to help them mentally rehearse for upcoming challenges, and it has improved their performance in a wide variety of areas, including sales, business leadership, weight loss, overall fitness, and relationships, just to name a few. This tool is simple and it works. While you may not be competing in athletic competitions, it certainly helps to develop the athlete's mentality in other areas of your life.

How to Mentally Rehearse

1. Find a place where you will not be interrupted for at least five minutes. Sit down and begin to allow yourself to be in a relaxed state mentally, emotionally, and physically.

2. Pick a specific part of your day where you would like to achieve a positive result, such as a meeting, test, or appointment.

3. Imagine yourself going through the activity step by step, from your own perspective rather than a third-person perspective. Visualize yourself handling all of the challenges that may arise with ease, moving from one challenge to the next without any negative effects on your performance. Continue to see yourself successfully going through the actions it takes to achieve the results you are after.

4. As you complete the actions, see yourself being victorious and achieving the desired outcomes. Make sure to celebrate the victory and experience all of the positive thoughts, feelings, and emotions that will occur when you are victorious.

Repeat this process before all of the important events in your day. Each time, see if you can find a way to amplify the experience by activating more of your senses, such as sight, touch, taste, smell, and sound. The goal is to incorporate sensory experience into the mental rehearsals so they are more realistic, and thus effective.

LIVE IT CHALLENGE

Mentally rehearse your day for five minutes each morning. Think about the big moments of your day and go through them step by step. Visualize yourself being successful and getting the results you're after.

The Power of Our Thoughts

"Miracles are not contrary to nature but only contrary to what we know about nature."

—*Saint Augustine*[2]

The power of our thoughts in changing the physical world has long been debated in cultures all over the globe. People hope and pray for certain outcomes, spend time meditating, and hold positive intentions, but does that make an impact on what actually happens, or just make us feel better? When it comes to scientifically proving that desired outcomes are a result of our thoughts nudging them in a certain direction rather than a happy coincidence, we've come up short. That is, until recently.

Numerous studies have been conducted on "directed remote mental influence," or psychokinesis, which in simple terms means the power of intention. In millions of trials, scientists have proven that thoughts do, in fact, affect the physical world, such as living organisms, objects, and machines. In the book *The Intention Experiment*, Lynne McTaggart explains this field of study and the implications it has on how we think about the physical world.[3] Her findings are remarkable because they tie to both quantum physics and the spiritual world, two realms that have historically appeared disconnected.

One study asked people to concentrate on picking one outcome over the other in a trial that should yield fifty-fifty results. This was done with a computer that generated one picture or the other, randomly and repeatedly. Essentially, a computerized coin flip. Participants were told to focus on one outcome to see if they could influence it to occur more often. Through more than 2.5 million trials conducted by sixty-eight independent researchers, results showed that thinking about a certain answer made it appear more often.

A different study focused on the power of positive thinking, negative thinking, and ignoring something altogether. Masaru Emoto, a researcher and alternative healer from Japan, tested the power human thoughts have on preserving white rice in water.[4] Since humans are 60 percent water, he wanted to see if human thoughts could affect the rice and water combination. If so, it would show it's likely that thoughts affect our bodies on a physical level as well. Emoto put equal amounts of cooked white rice and water in three different containers, and directed different emotions at these containers over thirty days. He thanked the first container, told the second container it was a fool, and ignored the third container. Sure enough, after thirty days, the containers of rice were vastly different from one another. The rice that was thanked was fermenting and emitting a pleasant odor. The rice that was told it was a fool was rotting. The rice that was ignored was rotting even more. If this sounds hard to believe, you aren't alone in having that thought. Emoto's experiment got attention on the Internet, and many skeptics have tried it out for themselves over various lengths of time, posting photos that match Emoto's results, as well as their surprise that the experiment actually did what he claimed.

These results are extremely powerful, because they prove that human thoughts affect the physical world. If our intentions have been proven to affect both machines and living organisms, imagine what's possible in terms of our emotions contributing to the world around us. Both our positive and negative emotions could actually be contagious in a literal sense. What we expect to happen might contribute to getting that exact result. It's mind-blowing to think about.

While there is certainly still a lot to learn about the power of human intentions, it is in our best interest to use the limited knowledge we have to our advantage. Whether you choose to pray, meditate, or hold positive intentions, you now have the scientific proof that your thoughts are more than just thoughts. How much more is yet to be uncovered, but it's smart to use every advantage you possibly can to achieve the results you want.

Remember, though, that life supports that which supports life. You can see this present in the world around us—living organisms thrive by contributing to the growth of other living organisms, whether the same species, a different species, or both. It's what keeps the planet and the organisms that inhabit it evolving and thriving in the long term. When you focus your positive intentions toward others instead of just on yourself, you can tap into the energy around you, whether you want to call it Mother Nature, God, or simply the universe. This universal energy intensifies when numerous people are focusing their efforts toward the same intentions or praying for the same things. If one person's thoughts can impact the physical world, it's compelling to consider what hundreds of people, or even thousands, can do. The nudge that people create with their minds could turn into more of a shove with our combined energy. While some of this theory is from deductive reasoning rather than scientific evidence, thinking about what's possible with the power of our minds is truly fascinating.

Although your mental strength may be the strongest when it's directed at helping others, this isn't to say you can't focus your efforts toward your own needs sometimes. In fact, when you think about the challenges ahead of you, you *should* hold intentions, pray, meditate, or do whatever else brings you mental strength. When you do this, however, make sure it isn't a substitute for taking action. There are too many people nowadays who believe if they just sit down and think about the outcome they want and how amazing it is, then it will show up in their lives. It doesn't work like that. Just like Muhammad Ali doing his mental rehearsals, you still need to have a clear set of actions that you are willing to take to reach your goals. Now here's the caveat: these actions do not have to be everything that has to happen to create the results. They can simply be all that you know you are capable of doing at that moment. For example, you may not know how to start a business, take it public, and become a billion-dollar company, yet you do know the day-to-day steps for the beginning segments of this process. That's where your intention has to lie. The long-term vision or desire can be to take it to that million- or billion-dollar goal you want to reach, but your intention must be the action steps you are going to take daily to lead to the results you desire and deserve.

Remember to focus on more than just yourself, especially in the power of prayer, meditation, and intention. Yes, spend time focusing on overcoming your own challenges and achieving the results you are after, but the more you focus on helping and serving others, the more life force will get behind and assist you in achieving the results you are truly after.

LIVE IT CHALLENGE

Use prayer and meditation to clear your mind and prepare for the actions you are about to take. Each day, spend ten to twenty minutes clearing your mind and saying a prayer, meditating, or defining the intention you set forth for that day or the following day, depending on what time of day you do this. Regardless of whether you are praying about it, meditating about it, or just setting the intention itself, make sure to set it with a clear plan of action.

After reading this chapter, you should have a much better understanding of the incredible results you can achieve by harnessing your mental strength. I'm sure you're ready to go out there and try these strategies and tools yourself, but don't forget one important thing. While the power of mental strength is inspiring, it is not a substitute for physical practice. Success starts in your mind, but you still need to apply yourself physically by taking consistent action. It's a balance between mind and body that you can master through hard work and dedication.

CHAPTER 11:

RAISING YOUR STANDARDS

"I refuse to lower my standards to accommodate those who refuse to raise theirs."
—*Steve Gamlin*[1]

I grew up hearing my dad share the philosophy of "raising standards" over and over again. It was a key in his own life to transforming himself personally and professionally. He said, "If you don't set baseline standards for what you'll accept in your life, you'll find it easy to slip into behaviors and attitudes and a quality of life that's far below what you deserve." The key is to raise the bar on what you are willing to accept in life.[2]

If you look around in your current life, almost everything you see (good and bad) is a reflection of your personal standards. The way you dress, the people you spend time with, the job you have, the current balance of your bank account, and so on. They are all a reflection of the standards you hold for yourself either consciously or subconsciously. If you aren't 100 percent happy with all of these aspects of your life, it's time to raise your standards. The first key in this process is to think back to Chapters 2 and 3 (the majors) and ask yourself:

Is there any specific area of my life that is not where I want it to be?

The truth is that all people have some areas of their lives where they would like to see improvement. Throughout my many years of running workshops and training sessions around the world, I have met only one man—*one*—who considered himself to be a 10 out of 10 in all areas of his life. He was a ninety-four-year-old gold medalist who had competed in the Winter Olympics at Lake Placid, New York, in 1932. He stood up in a training session I was having at a real estate office in Florida and blurted out, "I am all 10s." I immediately asked him what his secret was to being all 10s. He said, "Son, when you get to my age, you realize that we are all 10s!" My only response was, "Sir, you've earned it."

Besides that man, every other person who has participated in one of my workshops has had some area of life where they would like to see improvement. Regardless of whether it is your health that is currently a 5 out of 10 or your relationships that are a 7.5 out of 10, if they are not at a 10, why not? What is keeping you from having those major areas of life be exactly the way you dream them to be in your Ideal Day vision?

Take a moment to write down the answer in your notebook, and keep it nearby for the rest of this workshop.

Four Steps to Raising Your Standards

Step 1—Beliefs

The very first step in raising your standards is identifying all of your current limiting and empowering beliefs. Limiting beliefs are the types of beliefs that keep you from reaching your goals, while empowering beliefs are the types that set you up for success.

Let's test your beliefs really quickly and figure out what you believe about your future.

Close your eyes and imagine what you will look, feel, and act like, and what you will be doing, at eighty-two years old.

- What do you see?

- How do you feel?

- How flexible and agile is your body?

- What kind of activities do you partake in every day?

- What are you excited about?

- What projects are you working on?

- What difference are you making in the community around you?

Did you visualize it? Good! Now let me introduce you to Sister Madonna Buder, the "Iron Nun."[3] She entered a convent at twenty-three years old and became a Catholic nun. She started training as an athlete at forty-eight years old. Her first triathlon was at fifty-two years old. She's already completed 325 triathlons. At seventy-five and seventy-six years old, she competed in the Ironman triathlon at Kailua-Kona, Hawaii. In 2012, she became the world record holder for the oldest person to complete an Ironman competition, at eighty-two years old. She was quoted saying, "I train religiously!"

Here's my question: Is this how you envision yourself at eighty-two years old?

Are you still physically active? Are you competing in races and testing your limits? Are you showing yourself physically, mentally, and spiritually what you are capable of? Or did you see yourself as an old, wrinkly person, sitting hunched over in a chair? Are you thinking, "Oh, my aching back," wondering what is for lunch today and how things are going over at the bridge club? Well, there's nothing wrong with those things, but I'll tell you this. Wherever you believe you are headed, that is where you are, in fact, headed. That's why you need to raise your standards. If you pictured yourself like most elderly people you have met, it's likely you are holding a limiting belief, which is the type of belief that will keep you from living your best possible life. If you see yourself as a young, fun, wild, adventurous, and passionate eighty-two-year-old, your mind, body, and emotions will find a way to get there. We talked about intention in the last chapter, and it's a real thing. If you see yourself as old, hunched over, and having limited mobility, that will become your reality.

Here's another chance; let's try it again. This time, imagine yourself at one hundred years old—a centenarian. With today's technology and modern medicine, living to one hundred is becoming possible for more and more people.

- At one hundred years old, how do you feel?

- How active are you?

- How agile are you?

- How flexible are you mentally, emotionally, physically, and spiritually?

- What are you focused on?

- What are you doing, and who is there?

Let me ask, did your vision change? I hope it did. You may still have seen an old, wrinkly person, or you may now see a young, fresh, excited, abundant, passionate centenarian.

Let's go to someone I learned about last year named Robert Marchand. He's a 102-year-old Frenchman who, in 2012, established a centenarian record for the fastest 100 kilometers (62.13 miles) on a bicycle. He set the record at an average speed of slightly more than 23 kilometers per hour (14.3 miles per hour), in Lyon, France.[4] In early 2013, he took it a step further and broke his own record.[5]

Let me ask you, is that what you see when you picture yourself at one hundred years old? Competing in world championships? Are you stretching the boundaries of the majors, such as business, finances, and your spiritual life? Mentally and emotionally, is that what you see for yourself at one hundred? Or again, did you see an aching older person who is hunched over and losing mobility? Many people say they dread growing old, but what they really dread is the image they hold of what an older person has to be—their limiting belief.

Remember, the belief you have about your future is where you're headed. So let me ask, when you think about the future, what do you imagine happening in your business, finances, relationships, health, and all the other major areas of your life? Is your mind flooded with empowering thoughts of all the amazing things you are going to accomplish, how incredible you are going to feel, and the unlimited possibilities that await in your future? Or when thinking about the future does your mind immediately flood with uncertainty, fear, and worry?

If your mind floods with empowering thoughts and images that fill you with passion and inspire you to take action each day, you have a bunch of empowering beliefs. Congratulations! These are a much-needed element in achieving rapid results. Empowering beliefs help you go out and put forth your best effort in turning your vision into reality.

Most people hold both limiting and empowering beliefs about various parts of their lives, which may change or fluctuate over time, sometimes even based on how they are feeling that day. It's key for you to examine the beliefs you hold and realize when limiting beliefs are holding you back. This is the first step in raising your standards. Take some time to review the following empowering beliefs and limiting beliefs, and see if any strike a chord with how you feel about yourself and your goals.

Empowering Beliefs:

- If they can do it, I can do it.

- I did it once, I can do it again.

- Anything is possible if I'm determined.

- I'll try my hardest, and I'll be in the best position for success.

- I'll find a way to make it work.

- I know I'll meet the right people along the way.

- I will learn whatever I need to know.

- This is the perfect time in my life.

Limiting Beliefs:

- I don't have enough time.

- I don't have enough money.

- I don't have the right education, background, or experience.

- I don't have the right connections.

- I don't know where to start.

- I'm too old/young.

- I'm too tall/short.

- I'm too skinny/fat.

After reviewing these, where do you stand? If the empowering beliefs resonate with you, that's great! Keep holding those thoughts. If the limiting beliefs resonate with you too, that's OK. It's important to recognize how you feel, so you can move forward.

Take a moment to write down the answer to the following question:

What is the number-one limiting belief that is holding you back and keeping you from turning your Ideal Day vision into reality?

If you are struggling to come up with any limiting beliefs you want to break through, you might want to use the limiting story we talked about in the LIVE IT Challenge in Chapter 8.

In some of my workshops, we help participants break through their limiting beliefs by using a physical metaphor. People write down their answer to the aforementioned question on a board, and on the other side of the board they write down all of the new empowering beliefs they would like to have replace that answer. Breaking the board becomes symbolic for breaking through their fear and releasing their old limiting beliefs. The experience has very little to do with the actual board and more to do with what we allow that board to represent for the person breaking it.

For example, less than a year ago, we were teaching our annual Rapid Results Retreat and had a session focused on breaking through old limiting beliefs. We had a woman on board who had a few beliefs that were tearing apart her life and making her feel like she had nothing to live for. Prior to joining the retreat, she had a series of unfortunate events happen all in a row. Her house burned down with everything she owned inside, so she hired a contractor and used her entire life savings to rebuild the house. That contractor took the money and skipped town, leaving her with no money, no house, and no way to take care of her son who lived with her. She got insurance money for the house, but she chose to give it to the contractors who had been working on her house but who had never gotten paid from the guy who stole the money. As you can imagine, she was in a tough spot in her life. The limiting beliefs she had stuck in her head were "People are horrible," "I can't trust anyone," and "I have nothing in life left to live for."

On the very last day, when we were doing a recap and asking all of our participants about their experience during the retreat, she stood up and let us know that when she boarded the ship she had no plans of returning. She had set everything up at home so that she wouldn't be missed, and she had decided to go see a few beautiful countries and somewhere along the journey toss herself off the back of the ship and end her life. She told us that our session focusing on breaking through our old limiting beliefs saved her life. The goal of breaking boards was a physical metaphor that changed how she felt about herself and her future, and thankfully, she is alive today because of it.

I'm happy to say most people don't find themselves in this dire of a position during our workshops, but they still find the process of breaking through limiting beliefs to be the single greatest thing that pushes them forward. A friend attended one of our seminars in early 2013 and changed her life when she identified her limiting belief and broke through it. Instead of breaking boards, we used arrows. On the arrow she broke, she wrote down, "I'm afraid if I quit my job to run my business full-time, I won't make enough money and then I'll be in a worse position."

She had been working in marketing for several years and doing freelance marketing content on the side. She wanted to transition her business to full-time hours, but living in New York City, she was worried the income from a new business wouldn't be enough to support her financially. When she identified this belief as the single thing holding her back from the journey to her ideal life, it became clear what she had to do. She broke through the arrow and her limiting belief, and made a decision to raise her standards. She is now running a successful business and says she couldn't be happier.

Now that you've heard a few examples of other people's limiting beliefs, what's yours? Once you identify the stories or beliefs that are holding you back from raising your standards, you are ready to take the next step.

Step 2—Decision

The next step in raising your standards is to make a decision to no longer allow that old limiting belief or story to stand in your way and keep you from the results that you desire and deserve. In order to do this, you will need to better understand the true meaning of making a decision. Derived from Latin, the word *decision* historically meant "a literal cutting off," which has transformed over the years into describing an irrevocable act or resolution. Sometimes people confuse decisions with the repercussions of making decisions. This is an important distinction, because making a decision actually comes much earlier in the process than people often think. When we hear of someone being successful, we think it's because of a recent decision they made, when in actuality, their decision probably came years earlier and put them on the path to success.

A great example of this is when Austrian skydiver Felix Baumgartner ascended 128,100 feet above the earth in a stratospheric balloon and set the world record for the longest free fall.[6] You might remember hearing about this in 2012, since it made news around the world. Most media outlets covered the event in a way that made it seem as if Baumgartner's decision to make that jump had happened as he was hovering above the earth, just before he let go and started falling. People remarked on how brave he was in that moment to have been able to jump.

Baumgartner was certainly brave in achieving this feat, but his decision actually was made years earlier, when he decided to join the Red Bull Stratos team that organized the dangerous jump. He agreed to participate in the mission with the hope of helping to provide valuable medical and scientific research data. He knew that several people who had attempted a similar feat in the past had died in the process, but assuming it was humanly impossible was a limiting belief that Baumgartner wasn't willing to accept. His real decision was made when he decided the risk was worth taking. When he was hovering above earth, ready to take the final action on this particular journey, his decision had long been made. He had cut off other options, and he had put himself on the path to turn his ideal vision of skydiving from space into reality.

When we look at the situation this way, it's easier to see how making a decision is just the beginning of the journey. To make progress on achieving your dream life, you need to make a decision *now* so you can continue moving forward. Right now is your moment to make a decision to squash those old limiting stories and beliefs that have held you back in the past and free yourself from them once and for all.

Decisions That Changed the World

Most people never imagine how big of an impact one decision in their own lives can make on the world around them. Here are a few examples of people who stood up to their own limiting beliefs or the limitations that society attempted to place on them and changed the world in the process.

- Rosa Parks made the decision that she was tired of giving in to racial discrimination. On December 1, 1955, she was asked to give up her seat on the bus to a white passenger. Since she had already made her decision that she was tired of not standing up for herself and what she believed was right, she didn't get up. Her one decision to raise her personal standards caused a ripple effect across the country. It sparked the bus boycott in Montgomery, Alabama, a movement to fight racial segregation that gained national attention. Martin Luther King Jr. was an organizer for the boycott, which influenced him to become a leader of the civil rights movement. Parks's single decision changed an entire nation.[7]

- Mother Teresa believed that all people are worthy of love and affection, and she made a decision to dedicate her life to providing that love and affection to people who needed it. Her outreach in helping the poor served as an example to people around the world and changed the way people thought about helping others. By making the decision to raise her own personal standards, she helped other people in raising their standards as well.[8]

How far will your decision go?

Now it is your turn to shape history. What decision must you make today in order to raise your standards and break through the limiting belief that has been holding you back?

Step 3—Commitment

After making your decision to break through the limiting belief that has been holding you back, the next step in raising your standards is to commit to that decision. This may sound like a given, but many people today have a skewed view on what true commitment is all about. We live in a society where about 50 percent of all marriages end in divorce.[9] Today, the average person holds ten to fifteen jobs throughout a career.[10] Gone are the days when most people spent their whole adulthood in the same job and with the same partner. This shift in norms has changed the way people view commitment. I remember hearing about a time in history when a "spit handshake" was enough to make a transaction for buying or selling property or other goods. Nowadays if you don't have a written contract and lawyers to enforce it, people often don't think they are obligated to follow through. Even with contracts and lawyers, people still try to back out.

This zeitgeist becomes problematic when you make the decision to raise your standards. Without taking commitment seriously, you could easily change your mind and go back on the decision that was crucial for you to break through your limiting belief and move forward.

Let me share with you my personal inspiration when it comes to true, lasting commitment. John Wooden is best known for his career as a college basketball coach at the University of California, Los Angeles, where he won ten NCAA championships. This job was his only college coaching job, and he stayed there for twenty-eight years. He taught players such as Bill Walton and Kareem Abdul-Jabbar what commitment is all about in basketball, but he held strong values for commitment in his personal life as well.

ESPN interviewed Wooden for a piece about his life in 2009, and his story struck a chord in my heart.[11] Wooden married his wife, Nellie, when they were both twenty-one. They were happily married for fifty-three years when she passed away in 1985 from cancer at age seventy-three. Wooden had the mixed blessing of living twenty-five years longer than the love of his life. In the ESPN interview, he talked about how he was still very much in love with his late wife. In fact, he had been writing Nellie a love letter every month since her passing, on the twenty-first, which was the monthly anniversary of her death. No one gets to read the letters, but Wooden said they say things like "Honey, I miss you more than ever. Our love is still there and I am still keeping my promise. There will never be another."

You Have to Take More Shots to Make More Shots

Michael Jordan is widely considered to be one of the best basketball players in history, if not *the* best. His success has been so widely celebrated, we forget that he's gone through low points just like everyone else.

"I've missed more than 9,000 shots in my career. I've lost almost 300 games. 26 times I've been trusted to take the game winning shot and missed. I've failed over and over and over again in my life and that is why I succeed."

—*Michael Jordan*[14]

This is a man who knew about commitment. He knew who the love of his life was, and that feeling didn't waver after not seeing her for years. He showed commitment in other areas of his life as well. He lived in the same city for sixty-one years. He decided to stop drinking in 1932 and never had a drop after that. He had his first kiss with Nellie when they were fourteen, and she was the only woman he ever kissed. He was a man who knew what he wanted, and he had the strength to follow through with his commitments. The interview is so emotionally moving that I challenge you to watch it without crying.

Wooden's love story is so rare that we sometimes forget this level of commitment exists outside of books and movies. But it does. Wooden's story is beautiful because he was 100 percent committed, and that commitment is what kept him strong all those years.

What has to happen for you to be 100 percent committed to breaking through that old limiting story once and for all?

Step 4—Action

This is the final step. If you have identified your old limiting beliefs, made a decision to cut them off, and are 100 percent committed, now the only thing left to do is take action and raise your standards! That may sound simple, but this is a step where many people struggle. Why? Well, there are a few reasons:

1. They didn't clear out their limiting beliefs.

2. They didn't commit 100 percent to the journey.

3. They took a small, wimpy action a couple of times and expected to get a world-class result. When that result didn't show up, they got frustrated and gave up.

There are two types of action you will need to identify to ensure you get meaningful results that last.

Focused Action

Focused action is typically the opposite of multitasking. But wait, isn't multitasking a good thing? Our society has certainly evolved in a way where multitasking is encouraged, and strong multitasking skills are even specifically asked for in job descriptions. However, that doesn't mean it's the best strategy for getting things done.

Business coach and author Dave Crenshaw says the power of multitasking is a lie. People think they can accomplish more by doing multiple things at a time, but they are actually *switchtasking*, meaning they are switching back and forth between tasks quickly. Switchtasking often has the opposite effect on productivity as people hope. Instead of getting more accomplished, switching back and forth makes people think and work slower, because they have to get acclimated to whatever they were doing before they took a break.[12]

As you take action toward your Ideal Day vision, focusing on doing a great job on one task at a time is a much better option than trying to do an OK job with a bunch of tasks. If something is worth doing in the first place, it's worth spending more time on it and doing it right.

Consistent Action

The more times you take action, the better your chances for getting the results you want. This may seem like a lot of work—because it is. Use your Emotional Rocket Fuel to stay motivated, so you take action every single day that will help move you closer to the life of your dreams. It's important to note that perseverance is key, since you are bound to take actions that don't immediately pan out exactly as you had hoped.

Thomas Edison is the perfect example of how taking consistent action makes a difference in the long run. Edison is most famous for inventing the lightbulb, but he and his team invented a variety of other products as well. What people don't always realize is that Edison tried thousands of ways to make things work before he had success. He said, "I have not failed 10,000 times. I have not failed once. I have succeeded in proving that those 10,000 ways will not work."[13]

Edison was successful because he was willing to take the consistent action needed for him to reach his goals. Are you willing to go after your Ideal Day vision and take action a thousand times without getting the result you want, and still keep trying?

It's Never Too Late to Take Action

Colonel Harland Sanders is best known for being the founder of Kentucky Fried Chicken, but he didn't start building his franchise business until he was sixty-five years old. He was past the age when many people retire, but he was faced with living the rest of his life on a small Social Security check or finding a way to keep earning a better living. He believed he deserved better and that his chicken recipe was so good that people all over the world would love it. He broke through the limiting belief that people thought he was too old to get started. He made the decision to go after his vision, and he committed to that decision. Over the next couple of years as he searched for business partners, he was turned down 1,009 times before he finally got to his first yes. His commitment was tested over and over, but he stayed true to following his dream and taking the actions necessary to bring Kentucky Fried Chicken to life. Needless to say, he was living on a lot more than Social Security checks as he enjoyed his golden years.[15]

This is a reminder that whenever you start working toward your dreams, it's still possible to turn your ideal life into reality.

LIVE IT CHALLENGE

- Think about the number-one limiting belief holding you back and keeping you from turning your Ideal Day vision into reality.

- What decision must you make today in order to raise your standards and break through the limiting belief that was holding you back?

- What has to happen for you to be 100 percent committed to breaking through that old limiting story once and for
all?

- What is one action you can take immediately to create
momentum toward rapid results in your life and business?

At this point in the process, I have seen people incredibly
pumped up and excited about their future. They feel charged up
and are ready to go out into the world and create their dream
lives. The next chapter is focused on helping you create your road
map to meaningful results to guide you throughout your journey.

CHAPTER 12:

IDEAL LIFE VISION

At the beginning of any journey, it's smart to map out all the different routes you could take to reach the destination, as well as about how long it should take you to get there. Along the journey, you will encounter roadblocks, detours, and other unexpected bumps in the road, so taking the time to create multiple routes will give you options when challenges arise. Instead of feeling crushed or doomed for failure when you face adversity, your road map will give you 100 percent certainty that you will reach the results you desire.

Let's start with creating your Ideal Life vision. It is similar to the process we used for the Ideal Day vision in Chapter 1, except this time we are going to expand that vision from a single day to many years. If you remember, we started with a single day in Chapter 1, because we wanted to create a snapshot of what it would be like to live your ideal life. Now that we've analyzed why you envisioned that day the way you did and gone through exercises on how to reach your goals, you're ready to fill in the blanks. By creating your Ideal Life vision, you will identify all of the things you want in life and gain a better understanding of when you would like to achieve those goals. From there, this vision serves as the road map that will guide you through life.

To create your Ideal Life vision, you will need to prepare just as you prepared in Chapter 1. Grab your pen and notebook, and make sure you are in a place where you won't be interrupted for the next thirty minutes or so. Allow your body to relax and try to quiet your mind, allowing the stress of the day to wash away. When you feel mentally ready to move forward, begin the following exercise.

Ideal Life Vision Exercise

Think back to your ideal day, as you first visualized it in Chapter 1. What would your life be like if you had lived that ideal day for twenty years? That's 240 months, 1,040 weeks, and about 7,300 ideal days. Settle into this vision and imagine what your life would be like after twenty years of having that experience. Think about how much you would have grown and learned throughout those twenty years. Push yourself to think even further ahead in your ideal vision than you ever have before. Who are you with? Where are you? How do you feel? What do you spend your time doing all day? Take five to ten minutes and write down everything you can think of that will be a part of your ideal day twenty years from now.

Once you have mapped out your ultimate Ideal Day vision for twenty years in the future and have identified everything that makes that day your ideal day, you are going to then focus on each of the majors in that day. Think about what specifically will be going on in each major category of your life, now that you've been living twenty years' worth of ideal days.

- What will your health be like twenty years from now?

- Emotional intelligence?

- Intimate relationships?

- Family

- Professional life?

- Finances?

- Spirituality?

Spend time going through each major category and create a crystal-clear set of goals for each of them.

We are going to consider these twenty-plus-year goals as the finish line for your marathon in life. This doesn't mean it's the end of your life, but it's the end vision for your current goals. The next step is to design the mile markers for your journey.

Let's work backward and break down the major progress points you will need to aim for in order to achieve your long-term vision. For example, if you imagined your finances being in a place where you no longer have to work and you're set to leave boatloads of money to your great-great-grandkids and favorite charities when you pass someday, what will you need to do over the years to shape your life to meet that vision? It's going to be hard to accumulate that kind of wealth overnight, so you need to have a plan. The same holds true for your health. If you envisioned being highly advanced in practicing yoga, you should map out a plan for getting those skills in the coming years of your life. Create specific and measurable goals that tie to your mile markers. Do this for all of the majors.

Next, we are going to get a little more granular. You have your mile markers, but we want to fill in the gaps to give you a better sense of direction. Think about all of the majors one by one, and create short-term goals for reaching your mile markers. Work backward from ten years out, then five, then one. An easy way to create a timeline for these goals is by breaking larger goals into smaller chunks, sometimes focusing on tasks you can accomplish in just a few months or less. Start with your ten-year plan for each of your major life categories and spend time writing out your goals.

Once you have your ten-year vision and goals, think back to what you would have to do in the next five years to be on track with those ten-year goals. Then repeat this process again by asking yourself, "What would I have to do in the next two years, one year, and six months to be on track with those future goals?" You want to continue this process until you are able to have a clear set of monthly, weekly, and daily actions that will assist you in achieving both your short-term goals and your overall Ideal Life vision. As we discussed in a previous chapter, smaller goals are more manageable, and checking progress regularly helps keep you on track. Mapping out the major milestones and vision you have for the next twenty-plus years of your life is one of the greatest gifts you can give yourself.

Along with your road map, you need the final few strategies that will assist you in turning your vision into reality!

Gathering the Best Tools and Resources

Now that you've completed your Ideal Life vision, you have probably noticed you need additional tools and resources in order to reach your goals. This can be as simple as reading books that teach you a new skill, asking a friend to help you, hiring a coach or trainer, attending a seminar, or getting help with child care so you have time to focus on your own needs. Alternatively, the tools and resources you need might be more complex, like getting a higher degree or a new job in a new field.

Whatever the scenario, make sure you don't underestimate the power of not only having the tools and resources that would help you, but having the best of what's out there. For example, if you want to go back to school, instead of picking the school closest to your house, vet your options and compare numerous schools. You shouldn't assume that all forward progress is equal; better resources will ultimately yield bigger steps forward.

If you aren't sure how to start doing your research to assess the quality of available resources, find people who have achieved the results you're after and learn from their experience. Don't be afraid to reach out to people you don't know yet and ask for their advice. This can be a great way to build new connections and find mentors. Successful people often enjoy helping people who are at earlier phases in reaching their goals, and you might be surprised how easy it is to get advice if you simply ask for it. When you connect with people who have done what you hope to do, figure out what they've studied and read, and with whom they've trained, so you can build a similar foundation for yourself. When you've gathered the best tools and resources you possibly can, it will help set you up for future success in crafting your ideal life.

Measure and Fine-Tune

You should consistently measure your progress to ensure you are staying on the right track. For example, if you were to drive across the country, it would be absolutely ridiculous to look at your map once, get on a road, and drive for a few days without ever checking to see if you were still on course. If you did that, you might start your trip from California with a goal of getting to Colorado and somehow end up in the middle of Texas. It would be extremely easy to veer off in the wrong direction and keep going a long way before you realized your error. By that point, it would be hard to get back on track, and you would have wasted a lot of time. The same holds true on your journey to your ideal life. Now that you have determined your milestones—the destinations on your life's journey—you need to consistently measure your progress to make sure you get to where you want to be, when you want to be there. Remember, you can't improve what you don't measure, because you won't know where you are in relation to the desired outcome.

Sometimes people are hesitant to measure their progress during their journey because they are afraid of addressing the fact that they are off track. If you do happen to go off track at some point, don't think of it as a failure, and definitely don't avoid addressing the issue. Measurement is simply feedback to help you understand where you are compared to where you want to be. If you find you are slow to make progress or you are moving further away from the results you desire, all you have to do is fine-tune your approach. Think of this process as regular maintenance, rather than a sign your plan is totally broken.

Think for a moment about your favorite guitarist—either a solo artist or someone in a band. You love this person and the music he or she creates. If someone were to give you a signed guitar this musician used, how valuable do you think it would be? I am guessing *very* valuable. What is the first thing you would want to do with the guitar? Play it if you know how or at least strum the strings to hear how it sounds. Since it just came from your favorite artist, imagine it was perfectly tuned—it would sound like heaven! Since you would want to protect your new prized possession, let's say you buy a cool case for it and display it in your house.

Six months later, an old friend comes to visit who loves that musical artist as much as you do. You show off the guitar and your friend goes nuts, so you decide to take it out of the case. You gently hand the guitar to your friend and see her face light up with joy. Since she is also a music lover, what do you imagine would be the first thing she would want to do with it? That's right, strum it! But after sitting in the case for six months, what do you think it would sound like? *Clang, bong, ching.* It emits some clunky, unpleasant, out-of-tune notes. At that moment, it would be ridiculous to snatch the guitar out of her hands, smash it on the ground, kick it across the room and yell, "What a sham, someone gifted me a broken guitar!" It would be equally ridiculous to take out a pair of scissors and cut off the strings that are out of tune. Why? Because the guitar isn't broken—it's just out of tune. To make it sound just as great as it once did, all you need to do is tune it.

This is a simple idea to grasp for guitars, but when it comes to people using the concept of fine-tuning in their own lives and businesses, most people go about it in all the wrong ways. They ignore or run away from anything in their lives that isn't the way they want it to be and instead focus on what is easy and comfortable. Anytime something doesn't work out, instead of fine-tuning that area of their lives, they just cut if off and ignore it. What a waste! All they need is a little fine-tuning on a consistent basis and they would be getting the results they dream of.

When your life needs fine-tuning, pick a new road or a new way to go after your goals. The key is to constantly check in and adjust your approach to keep yourself on track and making progress.

LIVE IT CHALLENGE

Set up a system to measure and fine-tune your life every day. Visit www.LiveItBook.com to grab a copy of our daily tracking workbook to help you measure and fine-tune your results daily.

Along with our daily tracking sheet, there are four questions you can ask yourself each day to help you capture the best part of your day, the greatest lessons of your day, and a way to become better tomorrow. These four quality questions are a key to constant daily improvement.

Go through these questions in this specific order to train your mind to look for what's right with your day and life first, instead of what's wrong. Remember, whatever you focus on in life, you get more of.

- What was great about today?

  - Spend a few moments noticing the top five things you can think of that were absolutely great about your day.

- What did I learn from today?

  - What were the greatest lessons from the day? Whether it's how to communicate with someone better, grow, inspire yourself, or take more action, how can you learn from today?

- What could I have done better?

  - Think about the majors in your life, and which of your actions didn't align with your goals 100 percent.

- How can I apply it tomorrow?

  - You should take action immediately! Take time to schedule this lesson into your daily action plan for tomorrow to make sure you're applying what you are learning. Not just learning it; remember: learn it and live it.

Allow for Grace

Through speaking at seminars and hosting workshops, I've learned that allowing for grace—taking comfort in doing all you possibly can—is often a controversial topic. When I get to this part of the program and start explaining what it's all about, some-times people shout out, "Finally, the good stuff!" or something enthusiastic along those lines. Other people groan and cross their arms because they see it as an insubstantial topic they think has no proof of making a difference, so they don't believe in it. Humor me and have an open mind as I explain how allowing for grace can give you peace of mind!

I am pretty sure that all of us have experienced this in action at some point in our lives. Think of a moment when you were working toward a specific goal, giving it everything you have, working 24-7 busting your butt, doing everything in your power to achieve the results you were after. As time ticked away and you soon found yourself getting closer and closer to the dead-line, there came a moment when you had done all that you are humanly capable of doing. You made all the calls, crossed all of your t's and dotted your i's, put in 110 percent effort, asked for help, constantly measured and fine-tuned, and were still pushing hard all the way down to the wire. And during those final few hours, you started to realize the control you thought you had over the outcome of the situation wasn't really control at all—you did your best, and that's all you could possibly do. You think about how if it's meant to be, it will be. You hope for the best and maybe say a prayer or ask the stars to align in your favor, but after that, all you can do is wait to see what will happen.

In that moment, grace steps in. It feels like magic; you are balancing on the precipice of either having something amazing or utterly disappointing happen, and suddenly, the phone call, letter, check, or exact person or information you needed shows up at just the right time to make all that you were working toward turn out in your favor. When you gave your all and put everything on the line, God, Mother Nature, the universe, destiny, or whatever else you want to call it kicked in and helped you get the results you were after. That is *divine grace*! It's one of those things that gives you tingles all over your body, because you are in awe of how perfectly everything fell into place. Sometimes people think of these occurrences as luck or coincidences, but I think it's more than that. When you think back to *The Intention Experiment* book we discussed earlier, it seems like we are just starting to get a scientific grasp on how our intentions can nudge outcomes. When you've done all you possibly can to influence the results you want, all you can do is allow for grace to step in and finish what you started. The crazy part I have come to realize about divine grace is that the more you notice it, acknowledge it, and believe in it, the more it will show up in your life!

LIVE IT CHALLENGE

Make an effort to notice divine grace more often, whether you want to call it Mother Nature, the universe, or God. Start by making a list of how divine grace has affected you in the past. Keep these times in mind as you keep an eye out for divine grace in the future.

Celebrate Your Success

This tip is simple, but it's a much-needed reminder. The more you celebrate your success, the more you will notice the positive things happening in your life. When you notice your success, you will be encouraged to keep going.

Most adults celebrate like old, boring adults. Maybe a pat on the back or a few words of congratulations, and it's on to the next thing. It's sad when you think about it. We have been trained to cover up or downplay how we feel and mask our positive emotions so that we don't upset others who aren't as excited about their own lives or results. In Australia they even have a name for this situation: *tall poppy syndrome*. This syndrome occurs when people get so tall, or successful, that they start to stick out, which threatens the people around them. The surrounding people, or flowers, don't like feeling subpar, so they cut the tall poppy down to size to show it isn't superior. This syndrome happens around the world in numerous cultures, even if there isn't a name for it. Sometimes people can't help but feel jealousy when others do well, which causes people to downplay their success and excitement over getting the results they worked so hard to achieve.

It's important to realize that you have the right to be happy and proud of your accomplishments! Wanting to celebrate your achievements doesn't mean you think you're better than other people or that you're seizing the opportunity to get the spotlight. The desire to celebrate is natural and healthy. Most importantly, having some kind of celebration will keep you motivated to achieve even greater results.

There are a lot of options to enjoy the mental benefits of celebration, but some are better than others. A lot of people nowadays choose to celebrate any type of accomplishment by going out for a drink. This is one of the strangest things I have ever heard of in my life. Instead of enjoying the incredible natural high that results from doing something amazing, people share in consuming depressants. Since going out for "a drink" easily turns into many drinks, celebrations frequently turn into something that makes people feel unlike their natural selves and maybe even sick the next day. It makes absolutely no sense at all. Instead of celebrating with vices, I challenge you to find options that feel good, are good for you, and good for others. Along with finding ways to celebrate that allow you to fully experience joy, I also challenge you to celebrate at 110 percent. Through your actions, you will inspire those around you to step up and celebrate their lives in healthy ways as well.

LIVE IT CHALLENGE

Celebrate—take time each day to celebrate all of the accomplishments that you have created in your life that day. No matter how big or small the accomplishments, make time to celebrate them fully!

Final Reflection

Our journey together is coming to a close, but your ideal life is just getting started. You have the knowledge you need to start radically transforming your life into anything and everything you want it to be. I know you will be shocked by what you can accomplish when you take consistent, focused action to reach your goals.

In my final thoughts to you, I want to share a short piece that Marianne Williamson wrote called "Our Deepest Fear" in her book *A Return to Love: Reflections on the Principles of "A Course in Miracles."*

> Our deepest fear is not that we are inadequate.
> Our deepest fear is that we are powerful beyond measure.
> It is our light not our darkness that most frightens us.
> We ask ourselves, who am I to be brilliant, gorgeous, talented and fabulous?
>
> Actually, who are you not to be?
> You are a child of God.
> Your playing small does not serve the world.
> There's nothing enlightened about shrinking so that other people won't feel insecure around you.
> We were born to make manifest the glory of God that is within us.
>
> It's not just in some of us; it's in everyone.
> And as we let our own light shine, we unconsciously give other people

permission to do the same.

As we are liberated from our own fear,

Our presence automatically liberates others.

With this in mind, I hope you will accept the challenge to learn, live, and give all that you can each and every day. I challenge you to strive to turn your dream life into reality. To spend time each day focused on measuring and fine-tuning the major areas of your life. To find a way to learn and grow as a person each and every day. To take all that you learn and live it in every way, shape, and form you can. To become the change you want to see in the world. And finally, I challenge you to give back and pay forward all you are humanly capable of each day. The greatest joy in the world is helping others. When you spend more time giving back, you'll find your dream life is closer than you thought.

ACKNOWLEDGMENTS

There are so many people who need to be acknowledged.

First, my beautiful and amazing wife, Amanda, thank you for all of your love and support!

Next, my father. Dad, thank you for all of your amazing support, guidance, insight, and coaching. Without all that you have shared with me, I would never have had the foundation for life and business that I have shared in this book. It would not have been possible without you. Thank you for believing in me, challenging me, and being my hero!

Mom and Grandma, you are my two favorite people in the world to talk to. You both have spent countless amounts of time and energy supporting me throughout my journey. Thank you for always being excited to hear my stories of traveling around the world and finding a way to make a positive difference. Thank you for continually helping me stay grounded and focused on serving others. And thank you for your never-ending love and support.

Grandma Nikki, thank you for teaching me to be 100 percent myself in every way, shape, and form!

Next, I have to thank everyone who was a part of my Semester at Sea program. Without this life-changing experience while I was in college, my eyes and heart would have never been opened to the world in such a special way. I want to take time to thank the team at the Institute for Shipboard Education office for all of its amazing work to help students experience the world. This voyage was a key factor in shaping who I am today.

And finally my amazing writing team. Amelia Forczak, thank you for helping me turn my thoughts and ideas into this amazing book. Maryann Karnich and Tammy Faxel, thank you for believing in me; the Learn it, Live it, Give it message; and this book. My hope is that it inspires millions of people around the world to live life to the fullest and turn their dreams into reality!

ABOUT THE AUTHOR

JAIREK ROBBINS was born in Santa Monica, California. He is a decorated performance coach and inspirational keynote speaker who has applied his innovative methods to living a life of adventure, philanthropy, and entrepreneurship. At the age of twenty-three, Robbins was awarded the Congressional Gold Medal from the United States Congress. By twenty-five, he gained international renown as the creator of a revolutionary approach to maximizing employee performance that accelerated organizational success for a wide range of businesses. He has a psychology degree from the University of San Diego.

Robbins's personal journey has included cage diving with great white sharks, white-water rafting down the Nile, encountering silverbacks in Rwanda, and working as a volunteer in underdeveloped regions. He supports a number of charities and nonprofits, such as the Students Partnership Worldwide and the Just Like My Child Foundation. He lives in Florida.

NOTES

Chapter 1

1. Brendon Burchard, *The Millionaire Messenger:Make a Difference and a Fortune Sharing Your Advice* (New York: Free Press, 2011), 140.

2. Dana R. Carney, Amy J. C. Cuddy, and Andy J. Yap, "Power Posing: Brief Nonverbal Displays Affect Neuroendocrine Levels and Risk Tolerance," *Psychological Science* 21, no. 10 (October 2010): 1363–1368.

3. Stuart Allison, email message to author, March 2014.

4. Janice De La Garza, email message to author, March 2014.

5. Victoria Boye, email message to author, March 2014.

Chapter 2

1. Jane McGonigal, "Gaming Can Make a Better World," TED Talk video, 20:03, filmed February 2010, http://www.ted.com/talks /jane_mcgonigal_gaming_can_make_a_better_world/transcript.

2. "Television Watching Statistics—Statistic Brain," 2013 Statistic Brain Institute, publishing as Statistic Brain, December 7, 2013, http://www.statisticbrain.com /television-watching-statistics/.

3. Tom Corley, "20 Things the Rich Do Every Day," *Dave Ramsey* (blog), accessed February 3, 2014, http://www.daveramsey.com/blog /20-things-the-rich-do-every-day.

4. Richard Weil, "Walking," MedicineNet.com, accessed May 19, 2014.

5. Gordon Houser, "How to Be Smarter (but without Shortcuts)," *Mennonite* (February 2012), 10.

6. John R. De Palma, "Laughter as Medicine," Hemodialysis, Inc. (website), June 2, 2002, http://www.hemodialysis-inc.com /readings/laughter.pdf.

Chapter 3

1. Garth Brooks, "Garth at Wynn Las Vegas," concert, Las Vegas, December 4, 2010.

2. Brian Warner, "How Walt Disney's Housekeeper Secretly Died a Multi-Millionaire," *Celebrity Networth*, July 1, 2013, http://wwwcelebritynetworth.com/articles/entertainment -articles/how-walt-disneys-30-year-houskeeper-died-a-multi millionaire/.

3. "About Nick" (bio of Nick Vujicic), Life without Limbs (website), accessed December 12, 2013, http://www.lifewith outlimbs.org/about-nick/bio/.

4. Nick Vujicic (speech at Rock Church, San Diego, July 29, 2013), http://kr.voicetube.tw/videos/print/9268.

Chapter 4

1. "About Team Hoyt: The Early Years," Team Hoyt (website), accessed December 12, 2013, http://www.teamhoyt.com/about/.

2. "Malala Yousafzai," *Biography.com*, accessed May 15, 2014, http://www.biography.com/people/malala-yousafzai-21362253.

3. "Nelson Rolihlahla Mandela," *Biography.com*, accessed May 15, 2014, http://www.biography.com/people/nelsonmandela-9397017.

Chapter 6

1. "Statistics: 100 People," 100 People: A World Portrait (website), accessed June 17, 2014, http://www.100people.org/statistics_100stats.php.

2. Malaria No More (website), accessed May 15, 2014, http://www.malarianomore.org.

3. Robert I. Fitzhenry, *The Harper Book of Quotations*, 3rd ed. (New York: Harper Perennial, 1993), 451.

Chapter 7

1. Aurelius, Marcus, The Meditations of the Emperor Marcus Aurelius Antoninus, bk. 12, tr. Francis Hutcheson and James Moore (Indianapolis: Liberty Fund, 2008)

2. Alex Korb, "The Grateful Brain: The Neuroscience of Giving Thanks," PreFrontal Nudity (blog), *Psychology Today*, November 20, 2012, http://www.psychologytoday.com/blog/prefrontal-nudity/201211/the-grateful-brain.

3. Morris Massey, *The People Puzzle: Understanding Yourself and Others* (Reston, VA: Reston Publishing, 1979), 9–17.

4. Steven Covey, *The 7 Habits of Highly Effective People: Powerful Lessons in Personal Change*, Anniversary ed. (New York: Simon & Schuster, 2013), 160–164.

5. Bronnie Ware, *The Top Five Regrets of the Dying: A Life Transformed by the Dearly Departing*, reprint ed. (Carlsbad, CA: Hay House, 2012).

Chapter 8

1. WHO/UNICEF Joint Water Supply and Sanitation Monitoring Programme, World Health Organization, and UNICEF, *Progress on drinking water and sanitation: 2012 update* (New York: UNICEF, 2012), 5, http://www.unicef.org/media/files/JMPreport2012.pdf.

2. "learned helplessness," Oxford Dictionaries (website), accessed May 18, 2014, http://www.oxforddictionaries.com/us/definition/american_english/learned-helplessness.

3. Alison Flood, "Potter Tops 400 Million Sales," *Bookseller* (website), June 17, 2008, http://www.thebookseller.com/news/potter-tops-400-million-sales.html.

4. Stephen McGinty, "The JK Rowling Story," *Scotsman*, June 16, 2003.

5. David R. Shaffer and Katherine Kipp, *Developmental Psychology: Childhood and Adolescence*, 9th ed. (California: Wadsworth Publishing, 2014), 124.

Chapter 10

1. Martha Beck, "What the Heck's a Vision Board—and How Can it Change Your Life?" *Oprah.com*, accessed November 27, 2013, http://www.oprah.com/spirit/How-to-Make-a-Vision-Board-Find-Your-Life-Ambition-Martha-Beck/2#ixzz2lsbn24vI).

2. "Miracles are not contrary to nature, but only contrary to what we know about nature," *The Quote Yard*, http://www.quoteyard.com/miracles-are-not-contrary-to-nature-but-only-contrary-to-what-we-know-about-nature/.

3. Lynne McTaggart, *The Intention Experiment* (New York: Free Press, 2007), 2542.

4. Masaru Emoto, "Scientific Proof Thoughts & Intentions Can Alter the World Around Us: Masaru Emoto's Rice Experiment," Higher Perspective (website), accessed February 6, 2014, http://altering-perspectives.com/2014/01/scientific-proof-thoughts-intentions-can-alter-physical-world-around-us.html.

Chapter 11

1. Steve Gamlin's Facebook page, posted November 11, 2011. Verified via email by Gamlin on May 12, 2014.

2. Anthony Robbins, *Awaken the Giant Within: How to Take Immediate Control of Your Mental, Emotional, Physical, and Financial Destiny!* (New York: Free Press, 1992), 35.

3. "Madonna Buder," *Wikipedia*, last modified May 18, 2014, http://en.wikipedia.org/wiki/Madonna_Buder.

4. Agence France Presse, "Robert Marchand Sets New 100-kilometer Speed Record," *Velo News* (website), posted September 28, 2012, http://velonews.competitor.com/2012/09/news/robert-marchand-sets-new-100-kilometer-speed-record_240211.

5. Daniel McMahon, "102-Year-Old Cyclist Robert Marchand Sets World Record," *Time.com*, posted January 31, 2014, http://time.com/5695/102-year-old-cyclist-robert-marchand-sets-world-record/.

6. "What Is the Mission?" Red Bull Stratos (website), accessed November 29, 2013, http://www.redbullstratos.com/the-mission/what-is-the-mission/.

"Felix Baumgartner," *Wikipedia*, last modified May 18, 2014, http://en.wikipedia.org/wiki/Felix_Baumgartner.

7. "Rosa Parks," *Biography Online*, accessed November 29, 2013, http://www.biographyonline.net/humanitarian/rosa-parks.html.

8. "Mother Teresa," *Biography Online*, accessed November 29, 2013, http://www.biographyonline.net/nobelprize/mother_teresa.html.

9. Jessica Ruane, "Divorce in America," Crime Wire (website), May 23, 2013, http://blog.instantcheckmate.com /divorce-in-america/.

10. Alison Doyle, "How Often Do People Change Jobs?" *About.com*, accessed June 18, 2014, http://jobsearch.about.com /od/employmentinformation/f/change-jobs.htm.

11. "John Wooden Love Letters," originally broadcast on ESPN, uploaded November 27, 2009, http://www.youtube.com /watch?v=tySxPue9Dmw.

12. Dave Crenshaw, *The Myth of Multitasking: How Doing It All Gets Nothing Done* (New Jersey: Jossey-Bass, 2008), 11.

13. Nathan Furr, "How Failure Taught Edison to Repeatedly Innovate," Forbes.com, June 9, 2011, http://www.forbes.com/sites/nathanfurr/2011/06/09 /how-failure-taught-edison-to-repeatedly-innovate/.

14. Michael Jordan, Nike commercial, written by Jamie Barrett from quote adapted from interviews with Jordan, 1997, http://articles.chicagotribune.com/1997-05-19/news /9705190096_1_nike-mere-rumor-driver-s-license.

15. Deepak (Yahoo Contributor), "Colonel Sanders' Relentless Perserverance Toward Success," *Yahoo Voices*, February 13, 2007, http://voices.yahoo.com/colonel-sanders-relentless-perse verance-towards-success-193399.html.